CREATIVE JEWELRY

A PRACTICAL GUIDE

CREATIVE JEWELRY

A PRACTICAL GUIDE

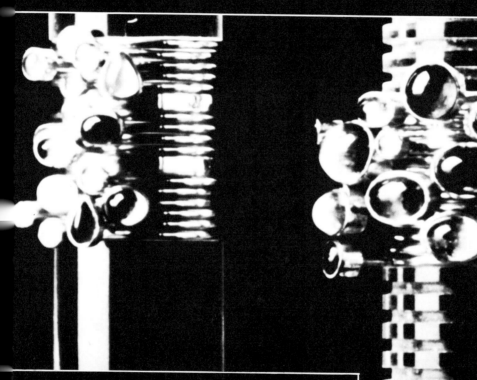

PATTI CLARKE

TAPLINGER
PUBLISHING COMPANY

opposite
Bracelet called 'Warrior'
made from ebony, beetle wings and a garnet bead.
Designed by Barbara Jardine

For my parents

Acknowledgements

I would like to thank the many institutions and
individuals for their help with the photographs.
Amongst them are
The Crafts Advisory Committee, Goldsmiths Hall,
The Royal College of Art, Brian Beasley,
Ian Haigh, David Ward and Ian Hessenburg
I would also like to thank my designer colleagues
and friends who have been kind enough to entrust
me with their work to be photographed.

A Studio Vista book published by
Cassell & Co. Ltd.
35 Red Lion Square, London WC1R 4SG
and at Sydney, Auckland, Toronto, Johannesburg,
an affiliate of
the Macmillan Publishing Co. Inc.,
New York

First published in the United States in 1978 by
TAPLINGER PUBLISHING CO., INC.
New York, New York

Library of Congress Catalog Card Number: 77-90127

ISBN 0-8008-1995-0

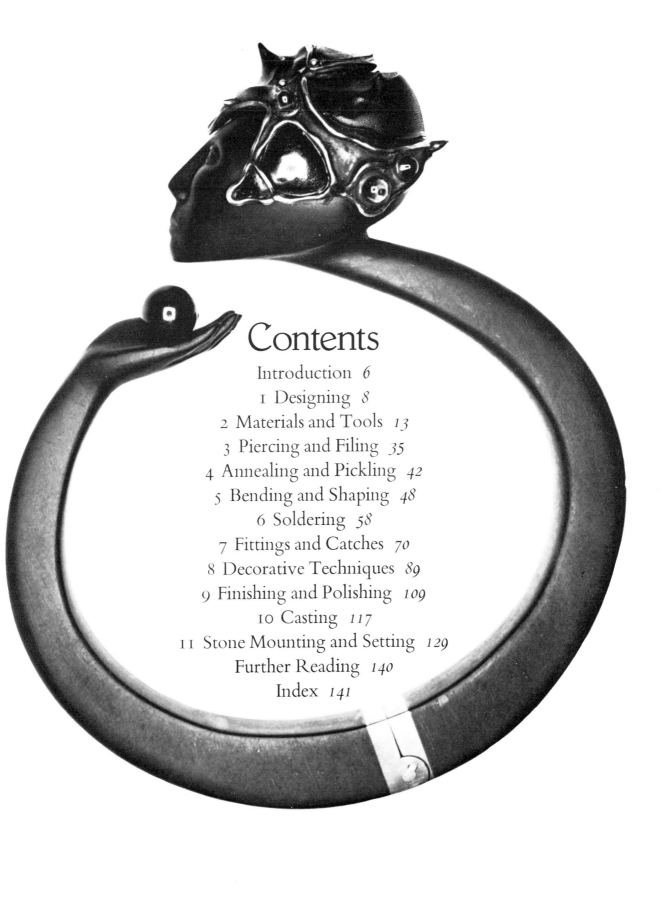

Contents

Introduction

This book is intended to be a fairly comprehensive guide to the techniques needed to be mastered in order to practise as a jeweller. I hope that both complete beginners and more advanced craftsmen will find something of interest and value, as the book covers both basic materials and techniques and the use of some of the more unusual materials popular with modern craftsmen.

I have started with a chapter on design, hopefully introducing some people to the idea that creating is more satisfying than copying. With a little time and thought the mental technique of design can be accomplished as easily as any physical technique. For the purposes of easier explanation and comprehension, step-by-step illustrations are sometimes given throughout the book. These are used only as a vehicle for explanation, and it is not intended that the designs should be copied—never look upon anything as just a technical exercise. Seize the opportunity to use your creative talents and design something of your own, even if it is only to practise a new technique.

The book then continues by outlining the basic workshop and essential tools, although it is also possible to work on an ordinary table with very few tools. With the help of illustrations I have tried to cover most of the techniques that a jeweller would use. Today the dividing line between a jeweller and a silversmith or goldsmith has become very blurred, with each using the other's techniques – which is as it should be. Thus by reading books on silversmithing you can learn of useful techniques such as spinning and raising. If your attitude towards the crafts remains flexible, you will continually find techniques attributable to other crafts which can be incorporated into your own work. The use of macramé and other textile techniques in wirework is just one example.

If you already have some mastery in jewelry, you may disagree with some of the ways in which I do things – I often find I disagree with other jewellers' methods and there is always more than one approach. Again, be flexible – try all the methods that you come across and keep to the one that you find easiest and quickest. Some techniques seem to take a long time before any appreciable result is achieved, particularly in the area of finishing and polishing. This can be very irritating when you are eager to get on, and there is a temptation either to skip a stage, thinking it won't show, or to search for a piece of machinery to do the job for you. In the first instance, the missed step usually does show – although you may shut your eyes to it at the time, several months later it will suddenly be very noticeable. In the second instance, fast-moving machinery tends to move too fast, leaving you with even more work to do to rectify the damage.

Oxidized silver and bead necklace. Designed by Lexi Dick

So you should learn to come to terms with and accept the occasional tedious job.

Throughout the book photographs of famous and not-so-famous jewellers' work have been used to illustrate both modern design and the use of some of the materials and techniques. You will notice that there is a variety of design, and that whereas some work uses only one material and a few techniques, others may use many materials or techniques. It is just this kind of flexibility and variety that you should try to achieve to make your own work modern, varied and exciting.

1
Designing

It is not by accident that the first chapter in this book is on the subject of design. We cannot begin to make anything until we know what it is we want to make. For centuries now there have been arguments between artists and artisans as to which is the most important – the designing or the making. In fact the two should be indivisible. No amount of skill or craftsmanship can make an ill-conceived design into anything more than just that. Equally, an exciting idea would have great difficulty in bursting through a morass of bad workmanship. A sweeping curve will lose its sense of movement if it is translated by bad filing into a feeble, wavering line; sharp angles and taut, straight edges will lose their bite if they have been softened by sloppy polishing.

One of the most important things that you should develop is a high sense of standard. Do not be tempted to be lazy and think that just because you are learning it does not matter if the angle is not quite square, or there is still the odd scratch on what should be a highly polished surface. It *does* matter; there is very little point, and certainly no sense of pride or achievement, in doing something that is not to the very best of your ability.

However, the question is whether to learn to design or to make first, because unfortunately it is impossible to begin by doing both – you can take alternate steps in

each direction, but where should you take the first step? I believe implicitly that it should be taken in the direction of design. Teach yourself to see, appraise and think, and then apply the rule that whatever piece of jewelry you can conjure up in your imagination can be made some way or another. Do not worry initially about how you are going to make it; you are limited enough without adding to your limitations by only designing things that you know how to make.

The path you are following should thus widen, not diminish – design whatever you like and then learn how to make it. That way the quest for new techniques will follow naturally along your own personal path and not someone else's.

This does not mean that if you already know all about the working properties of the materials you are using that you should abandon this knowledge. Hopefully what should eventually happen, is that as you progress as both craftsman and designer, the two abilities should work together so that as you design you are aware in the back of your mind of how you are going to make your designs.

Unfortunately, to many people the word 'design' has many intimidating connotations – they feel that only 'talented' people can design. Every single person has the capacity to create and design something original to them; it is just that they may never have been

Silver brooch based on a cross-section of a cabbage. Designed by Polly Upham

called upon before to exercise it in this particular way. Every time you buy something – clothes, a car, or whatever – you are making design decisions. Apart from the considerations of need and economy, you usually buy something because you like it. Try to analyse why you like it – is it the shape, the colour, the texture that you like? What do you base your judgement on? You will usually find that your criteria come as a result of evaluating and comparing the assets and characteristics of one product against another. This is the very same process by which you design. If you design by drawing you make a mark and look at it; if you like it, you keep it, if not, then you change it until you do.

You need not use drawing as the vehicle for your design process, though it is by far the quickest method. You may prefer to make models out of paper, card, plasticine, or whatever you feel might help. However, if you can, try and develop skill with a pencil,

or any other drawing instrument. Drawing enables you very quickly to try out and evaluate ideas – almost as soon as the idea enters your head you can represent it visually for you to criticize. It is not necessary to make finished, polished drawings; as long as the marks indicate to you an idea of what it is that you are thinking about and enable you to organize your thoughts, that is all that is necessary. If you had to present drawings to a client, then it would be a different matter. Presentation drawings, as they are called, do precisely that – present to the client an easily assimilated image of the proposed design.

If you have never designed formally before, then you may well feel rather lost and not know just how to begin. No one can create something from nothing – you will have to feed your mind with images and experiences which you can use as a reservoir to draw upon. When you have established this reservoir, which you must continually top up, then you must learn how to be critical and discriminating – to discard some things and select others. Your faculty for discrimination can only be built up by evaluating your experiences. One of the best ways to develop this power is to go to museums and look at the examples of work there. You will see some of the best examples of design and craftsmanship. You will also see work that has the characteristics of widely varying influences – jewelry, especially in more primitive areas, was designed to have symbolic characteristics ranging from mythological to sexual.

Go also to the many admirable galleries and design centres that there are today showing what other people believe to be the best examples of modern design. By continually looking and comparing, you will quickly learn how to criticize and analyse constructively.

As time goes on you may find that the work you design has a similarity to other contemporary work that you see. This does not mean that you are imitating or not being original. We are all born and living in the same era, all subject to its experiences, influences, vagaries and whims of fashion, so it is hardly surprising that the results should be sympathetic. As for originality, some people claim that nothing is original, that it has all been done before. Although in some respects this is true, each individual is unique and even if the elements of his designs are composed of familiar forms he can still present them in his own original way. It is rather like cooking – although the basic ingredients have been in use for centuries, a different recipe will produce an original dish.

Just as you may think you are too much in sympathy with your contempories, do not despair if you seem to be out of step with them. This does not mean that the path you are following is any more right or wrong than theirs – it is simply your own. The most important thing is to have confidence in yourself and what you are doing, and the results will be better and certainly more original than if you try to adopt an alien style.

There are various ways in which you can feed the reservoir of your mind to stimulate you when you are designing. Some methods may appeal to you more than others and you should follow the direction in which you have the strongest response.

You may find the designs that appeal to you have organic characteristics – growing forms or meandering lines – in this case look to Nature for your stimulus. Look at flowers and their structure, take slices through cabbages, lemons, shells, poppy seedheads. Look at the texture and lines of geology, the stratifications in rock faces, the rounded, sea-

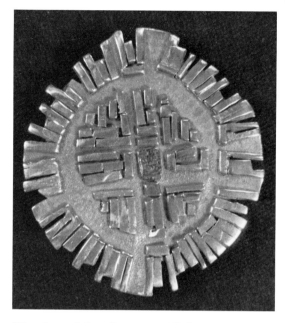

Silver brooch based on an aerial photograph of a city. Designed by Daphne Dinnage

washed form of pebbles, worm-eaten shells. Go to libraries and look at medical books – you may find the shapes and patterns of some viruses and obscure cross-sections of organs very interesting. Microscopic slides of cell structures can provide a wealth of patterns and forms.

If you find that more inorganic things interest you, then look at books on geometry, machine parts, printed circuits. You may find a stimulus in your surroundings, the view from a window, the structural organization of architecture, aeriel views of cities or the patchwork of fields and farms.

Instead of looking directly at other forms, you can just sit and doodle. Initially do not think too consciously about what you are drawing – you do not need to feel that every mark you make is a commitment. Scribble madly over a sheet of paper and then look at the results. Somewhere on the sheet there will be some marks that you respond to. Take these marks and work on them, discarding the aspects that you do not like and adding others – gradually an organized design will emerge.

You may prefer to work directly with the material that you are going to use. Take small pieces of varying thicknesses of metal sheet, bend them, fold them and see what forms evolve. In many ways paper is like metal, and you can use it to experiment with. Take lengths of different sections of wire, twist them, hammer them. You will find that the materials with which you are experimenting have characteristics of their own which may suggest ways in which you can use them.

You may have a stone or a piece of tortoiseshell with an interesting pattern that you would like to interpret. The patterns and shapes could provide a starting point for the design. A stone that has a crystalline lacy line across it may suggest using textured wires. The stone itself may have a strong shape that could be echoed in the design.

Perhaps you have a predeliction for movement and light, in which case you could design your jewelry as small feats of engineering with parts that move and wink in the dark and change colour according to the body temperature of the wearer.

When you have achieved a store of ideas, shapes, textures, forms, etc., then you have to decide how to use them because, after all, the purpose of all this is to design a piece of jewelry. If you have found a shape or pattern that interests you, try experimenting with it – make it larger or smaller, repeat it to make a scheme. A single shape that stands on its own as a pendant could be repeated to make a necklace. The shapes could be overlapped, or

placed with spaces between them. Shapes radiating from the centre like a sunburst or growing flower have long been one of the basic forms used by designers. Try texturing some areas of a design and leaving others plain, thus providing a contrast or a balance.

Contrast can play a very important part in designing. It can serve to accentuate parts of a design: areas of heavy modelling can be accentuated by plain, smooth areas; small areas of pattern, colour or texture could be the rich nucleus of a form. Contrast can be

Electron microscope photograph of a section through a tomato. This lacy effect could be achieved by imposing several layers of wire work. Photograph by Veronica Wright

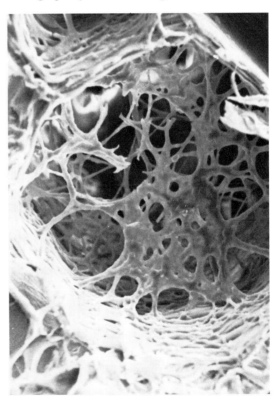

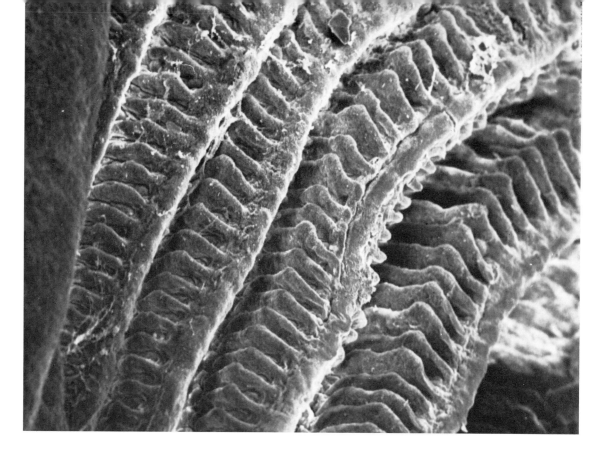

Electron microscope photograph of lamprey gill.
This ridged texture could be simulated by casting.
Photograph by Veronica Wright

---

used to create either a balance or a
disturbance. Although most of the time
designers try to achieve harmony and balance
in their designs, a slight disharmony can
prove arresting for the mind and eye. It is
rather like a discord in music – it has the
similar effect of calling some particular aspect
of the music or design to your attention.
However, discord and disharmony are purely
a matter of familiarity or the lack of it. After
you have listened to a discordant note many
times, its strangeness disappears and it no
longer seems disturbing. So what seems
discordant to you now may appear
completely harmonious in two years' time.

Just as plainness and texture can accentuate
each other, so can differing characteristics of
materials. The softness of wood could be
accentuated by the hardness of metal. The
qualities of a high polish can also affect a
piece of work. A highly polished surface will
make the shape appear smaller because
the reflective surface disappears into the
background. In the same way, an edge that
catches the light can seem stronger and more
important than an edge that does not. There
are many more characteristics that you can
employ to enrich your designs.

Fortunately, jewellers, unlike silversmiths,
do not have many functional characteristics
to consider. A brooch does not have to be
held or need a spout to pour from. Apart
from the mechanics of attaching the jewelry
to the body, it needs to be comfortable to
wear. Heavy pendants and razor-edged rings
are a little impractical. The most important
thing is that an article of jewelry should be
beautiful to the person who designs it and to
the person who wears it, for since time
immemorial jewelry has been used as a means
of beautifying the body.

2
Materials
and Tools

In designing and making jewelry, it is very likely that the materials you will most commonly use will be silver, gold and stones. However there are many other exciting materials that you could use, some of which are described in this chapter. Be adventurous with your materials because you may make discoveries of your own.

In the case of silver or gold, you may like to practise on other metals before going to the expense of buying the precious metals. Personally I am in favour of 'jumping straight in' and using whichever metal you like. Remember that when you use silver and gold, no matter what disaster may befall your piece of work, the metal is never totally lost. You may lose the fraction that you have filed away, but the main mass of metal can always be returned to your bullion dealer who will give you a fair price for your catastrophe. (It is more economical to save up all your scraps and take them back together.) So do not be dissuaded from using these precious metals just because you feel that you might be wasting your money. It is always more exciting to make the real thing rather than a mock-up or model and, besides, after you have spent many hours labouring over a model, your creative energies may well have been spent and the prospect of having to repeat yourself may be too tedious.

The following descriptions of various metals and their visual and working characteristics

will start with the most common and proceed to the more unusual ones. If you are technically minded, then such details as the melting points of different metals might interest you but remember that skill and practice will teach you to 'see' the changing temperature of the metal as you heat it.

METALS

Copper melting point 1083°C (1981°F)
Copper is a pinkish metal which is soft, malleable and ductile. This means that it can easily be bent or hammered into different shapes and can be drawn out into very fine thin wire. Unfortunately its malleability can also be a disadvantage because jewelry made from thin sheet or wire is easily squashed. Nevertheless, it is a good metal for a beginner, and because of its relative cheapness it can be used to practise on. To anneal the metal (for annealing see chapter 4), the metal is heated to a dull cherry red colour and then quenched in water. A thin flaky skin of black oxide forms on the surface of the heated metal (a reaction takes place between the copper and the oxygen in the air) but it is easily removed by pickling (see chapter 4).

Copper can be polished by the normal methods described in chapter 8. It is rather difficult to get a very high polish because the soft metal easily takes 'drag' marks from the polishing mops, so extra care has to be taken to move it round on the mops. Copper can be soldered easily, using ordinary silver solders, although obviously joints will show as a silver line. It is possible to get pink copper solders but they usually have to be ordered in large quantities.

Unfortunately this metal tarnishes quickly and needs to be protected by a layer of clear varnish, or alternatively chemically oxidized to produce another colour. (See chapter 8.)

Gilding Metal

This is a yellow-coloured metal which is an alloy of copper and zinc. Unless you particularly require the red tones of copper, then this is a better metal to use as it does not oxidize as badly when heated and is also harder. It can be worked in the methods described later in the book.

Nickel silver melting point 1445°C (2651°F)

This is a whitish metal also known as German silver, although in both cases the adjunct 'silver' is misleading as this metal is an alloy of copper, zinc and nickel. It is a much harder metal than those already mentioned and is also harder than silver. If it is worked 'cold' (i.e. without annealing), it can be made extremely resilient for springs and the snaps in box catches. It can also be worked according to the methods described later in the book.

Titanium

Titanium is an extremely hard metal which can only be bent with difficulty. It cannot be soldered to itself or to any other metal and is therefore usually riveted. Consequently it is best used in thin sheets, either flat or slightly curved. It can be finished by the methods described in chapter 8. The main attraction in using this metal is the beautiful colours that can be obtained by heating it. By gently playing a flame over the metal or heating it in a kiln, which gives more control, a wide range of colours can be achieved, ranging from straw yellow to pink-mauves and the most beautiful vibrant blue. The colouring is only on the surface of the metal and can easily be removed by rubbing with emery paper or with hydrofluoric acid. It you want to achieve more control over the colour variations, you can do this either with a thermostatically controlled kiln or by passing a small electrical current through the metal from an ordinary 12-volt battery.

Silver melting point 960·5°C (1760·9°F) Sterling 893°C (1671°F)

Silver is a beautiful, warm white metal. It is extremely malleable and ductile, and of all the metals mentioned here it is probably the one you will use the most. It can be worked according to the techniques described later in the book, and can be polished to give an extremely reflective mirror-like finish. Although it does tarnish, the surface will remain bright for some considerable time and with the many cleaning preparations on the market today it is relatively easy to clean.

Silver is most readily available in two forms – Britannia silver which is 95·8% fine silver, the other percentage usually being copper, and sterling silver which is 92·5% fine silver. As a general rule you should use sterling silver, unless you require the particular qualities of Britannia silver which is softer and whiter than sterling. There are also several special alloys available for particular techniques, such as enamelling, spinning or raising. The bullion dealer where you purchase your metal should have a catalogue

Necklace of oxidized silver, ivory and braid. Designed by David Courts

of the various alloys he manufactures.

Not only can you buy your silver in differing qualities, you can also buy it in differing forms. In less modern times you would have had to mix your own alloys and make them into whatever form you required. Today the highly specialized bullion manufacturers provide silver in various forms:

sheet in various thicknesses

wire in various thicknesses and sections – square, rectangular, round, triangular, D-shaped, etc.

tube again in various sizes and sections and also with different wall thickness. Usually sold in minimum 305 mm (12 in) lengths.

grain or shot for casting

Some firms even supply hollow beads, chains and various jewellers' findings (i.e. brooch, earring and necklace fittings) as well as claw settings for stones.

If you need something special and in a fairly large quantity your bullion dealer may be able to help you. Dealers also usually supply the various solders that you will need and some firms even supply information regarding the working characteristics of their metals. You pay for your silver by weight, with an added finishing charge for jewellers' findings and chains.

Silver, like copper and gilding metal, hardens through being worked and needs to be annealed. It can easily be finished and polished as described in chapter 8. If you want to know if a particular piece of metal that you have is silver, you can make a quick test by exposing some of the clean metal by filing the surface and then adding a drop of nitric acid. Pure silver makes a white froth, sterling silver will give a slightly more yellow one. Nickel and silver-plated copper make a dirty green froth.

Gold melting point 1063°C (1945°F)

Gold in its natural form is a beautiful, warm yellow metal and has always been extremely popular with craftsmen because of its fine working qualities. It is the most malleable and ductile of all metals, and can be hammered from a thick sheet to a thin tissue known as gold leaf. As a wire it can be drawn out as fine as a hair. It does not oxidize and is extremely resistant to corrosion by chemicals, and it can be polished to a high mirror-like finish with a deep reflection. Pure, or fine gold as it is called, is too soft to be used in its natural state, except for inlay work, so it is usually alloyed with small quantities of other metals to produce different qualities and colours of gold. This also alters the working characteristics, so it is wise to consult the manufacturer's catalogue on his own particular alloy. Yellow gold is made by the addition of silver and copper, red gold by the addition of copper, green gold by the addition of silver, cadmium and zinc, and white gold by the addition of palladium or platinum. Unlike the other gold alloys, white gold is rather difficult to work and will crack easily if abused.

In addition to being made in different colours, gold can also be made in different qualities known as carats – pure gold being 24 carat. Thus 18 carat gold is 18 parts gold and 6 parts of some other metal. In England, the most commonly used carats are 9, 14, 18 and 22. Like silver, gold can be bought in many different forms – sheet, wire, rod, tube and grain – and you can choose the form and quality best suited to your design and pocket. To solder your gold you must use the relevant solders, i.e. if you are using 18 carat white gold then you must use 18 carat white gold solder of the melting temperature that you require (see chapter 6 on soldering).

Platinum melting point 1773·5°C (3224·3°F)

Platinum is a relatively newly discovered metal which has only been in use for the last 150 years. It has many residues which are more rarely used, rhodium and palladium being two of them. Platinum has a bright bluish white colour and is quite easy to use. It is malleable and ductile and can be polished to give a high lustre. Because it is hard and does not wear away easily, it is often used to make the claw setting for precious stones – it also has the advantage of making a diamond appear larger than it really is. As it is so expensive, it is not often used to make complete pieces of jewelry.

Steel

Steel is a greyish-white alloy of carbon and iron and is available as carbon steel or various alloys. It is very hard and brittle but nevertheless has many qualities that can appeal to a jeweller. The high carbon steel is the one that you would use if you wanted to make your own tools. Stainless steel is the alloy most commonly used in making jewelry – although very hard it can be tempered and, depending upon the thickness, bent to a varying degree. Although stainless steel can be welded this is not usually satisfactory in jewelry and it is best used in a design which does not require soldering. It can be bought in many shapes and dimensions; sheet, wire and tube.

NON-METALLIC MATERIALS

Ivory

This is a creamy-white organic material obtained from the tusks of elephants. Because it does come from an animal there is obviously a limit to the size and shape that you can buy. The widest section is probably about 150 mm (6 in). As the tusk gets further away from the tip, a dark central core appears which was the nerve cavity. Sometimes this core drops out as it expands and contracts at a different rate to the outer ivory, so it is best to avoid using it. Ivory has a beautiful cross-spiral pattern formed by the growth rings of the elephant. There is an outer ring and a more heavily patterned inner ring. As you shape a piece of ivory, these patterns act rather like contour rings and accentuate rises and falls by their concentration on the surface.

Ivory is rather easily affected by temperature and dislikes being exposed to extremes of heat and humidity, when it is liable to crack. The main supplier in England keeps his stock in deep cavernous cellars where the air is damp and the temperature even. If you are buying your ivory from him, do not take it suddenly into a centrally heated room, store it in an airtight tin. Ivory can be cut and pierced with jewellers' saws and can also be turned on a lathe. It can be carved with smaller hand-made versions of woodcarvers' tools, and it can also be shaped with burrs and grinders in a pendant drill. To remove scratches use a fine file – you will need a file card to free the file teeth of the ivory debris, which will tend to make the file bind. The final smoothing can be done with very fine wet and dry paper, or flour paper. To achieve the final polish the ivory can be buffed with polishing pads and toothpaste (see chapter 9 for details).

Ivory can be tinted pale colours by soaking it for several days in a strong cloth dye solution. The colour achieved is very pale and does not penetrate beyond the surface skin so a deep scratch will expose the white ivory beneath it, but nevertheless some very attractive results can be obtained. As ivory matures it takes on a deep yellow-brown

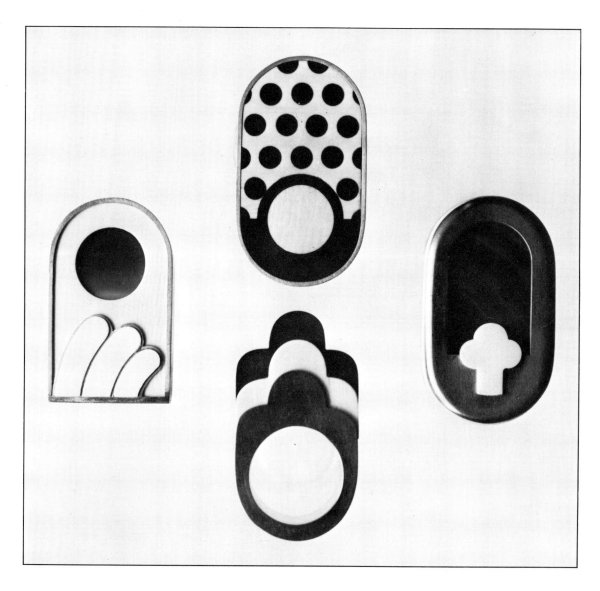

Jewelry designed by Cameron Duff
Left to right: 18 carat gold brooch with cornelian and ivory. Silver brooch inlaid with ebony and ivory. 18 carat gold brooch with cornelian and ivory
Bottom: 18 carat gold ring with cornelian and ivory

colour; it can also be prematurely aged by soaking it in a strong tea or coffee solution. Obviously ivory cannot be soldered but it can be joined by means of riveting, pegging or gluing. Of these, gluing is the least satisfactory as the two parts to be joined may contract and expand at different rates, thus placing a strain on the joint. For this reason too, pegs may work loose, though in practice this rarely happens. Metal rivets (silver or gold) or small screws are the best solution.

Tortoiseshell

This is another organic material, usually a semi-translucent reddish-brown colour with yellow patches. It is obtained from the shells of a specific breed of tortoise and is available in either thin, irregularly shaped sheets about 0·50 mm (1/64 in) thick or in blocks measuring approximately 130 mm × 80 mm × 6 mm (5 in × $3\frac{1}{4}$ in × $\frac{1}{4}$ in) which are made for the spectacle frame trade. The blocks are made of multiple sheets which have been glued, steam heated and pressed together.

Tortoiseshell is quite soft to work and can be sawn, pierced and carved like ivory. It has a more malleable quality than ivory, and boiling it in a salt solution makes it soft and pliable. It can then be moulded by trapping it between two prepared shaped pieces of wood, which are clamped together until the tortoiseshell is cool. If the shape has several changes of contour or section, it may be necessary to do this in gradual stages. The wooden formers should be perfectly smooth and polished, or the tortoiseshell may stick. The Victorians made many beautiful little snuffboxes by this method. Two or more pieces may be riveted or glued together using one of the epoxy resin glues available. Tortoiseshell can be finished and polished in the same way as ivory, and a final sheen can be achieved by rubbing it with a cloth impregnated with a thin oil such as linseed oil.

In view of the recent opinions concerning the conservation of these two organic materials, it will become increasingly difficult to buy them new, and you will either have to use old pieces or find a more acceptable substitute.

Amber

You may be able to find small lumps of raw amber, or you may have an old piece of amber jewelry that you would like to change. Amber is a form of resin and varies in colour from a semi-translucent pale yellow to a deep orange or brown. The more transparent and blemish free it is, the better quality it is supposed to be, but some of the marked pieces are more interesting. Often small fossilized specimens of animals or fern are entrapped in lumps of the resin. Amber is soft but brittle. It can easily be filed and sawn, but it may crack especially if it has inclusions. It can be finished and polished like ivory and tortoiseshell.

Abalone shell

Various shells can be used in jewelry and the most common of these is abalone. It has a pearlized finish of pale pinks, blues and mauves. You can buy either the whole shell or small pieces that have been prepared in some way or another for the larger users of shell, such as button manufacturers. The beautiful pearlized finish is present throughout the whole of the shell, once the green, dull outer surface has been filed away to expose the nacre. The inner sections of the shell have a more translucent and reflective quality than the outer edges, which are more opaque and less varied in colour. Abalone only reflects the light from certain directions, so that in a carved three-dimensional piece only certain areas will have the optimum brilliance. You should examine the reflective qualities of the shell before starting work or you may be disappointed with the results. If the shell is to be used in a flat sheet, then this problem will not occur as the reflective direction can easily be seen. Abalone is soft and brittle, but it can be filed and sawn. If you are sawing a thin sheet, take great care to

Bird necklace in silver and resin. Designed by
Susanna Heron

Silver, abalone shell and titanium brooch.
Designed by Catherine Mannheim

support the whole of the sheet, and sawing
should be done slowly and steadily to avoid
breaking the thin shell. It is best attached to
the metal jewelry by gluing or riveting.
Again, care must be taken when drilling
holes to prevent the edges from splintering –
a wise precaution is to stick adhesive tape
over the area to be drilled and then drill
through both materials. As abalone shell is
rather fragile, it is worth protecting the edges
from sudden knocks. It can be finished like
ivory.

Wood

You may wish to use wood in your jewelry,
and very interesting and attractive results can
be achieved by using it in conjunction with
metal. There are many different varieties of
wood, giving a wide range of both colour
and grain pattern, but basically they have the
same qualities. Wood can be sawn, filed and
carved, using the appropriate carpentry tools.
It can be joined to metal by screws, rivets or
epoxy resin glues. To finish and polish wood
see chapter 9.

Resin

Polyester resin is a relatively new material to
the jewelry field and one which has been used
successfully by many modern designers. The
resin itself is a clear syrupy liquid which,
when mixed with accelerators and hardeners,

turns to a solid plastic-type material. It can be mixed with various pigments to produce a wide range of opaque and transparent colours.

Some of the resins are supplied already mixed with the catalyst (hardener) and only need the addition of the accelerator. The colouring pigments also affect the hardening time and, although the resin suppliers supply a chart of the hardening time, this can only be used as a rough guide and you will need to experiment yourself. It normally takes about 2 hours to harden but is usable for much less than this – about 20 minutes. Once it has turned to jelly it must be abandoned. Mixed and coloured resin cannot be kept for re-use, so you should mix only what you need for each particular piece of jewelry.

As this material is quite difficult to remove from utensils, it is usually mixed in paper cups or other similar disposable containers. It should be stirred with glass rods, which can be cleaned, or disposable paper lollipop sticks.

Measure out the amount of resin that you need. Add the required pigment and stir carefully until it is well mixed – do not stir too violently or you will introduce bubbles which are very difficult to disperse. When the colour is correct, add the accelerator according to the manufacturer's instructions. The resin is now ready for use.

You can use resin in several different ways. It can be cast to reproduce forms, using either inflexible plaster moulds or flexible moulds such as vinamold or cold-cure silastimer, which have the advantage of being re-usable. The moulds have to be painted with a parting agent which will readily release the cast from the mould after it has cured. There are different kinds of parting agents and mould materials available, and you should consult your suppliers. The resin is poured into the prepared mould and left to cure.

Resin can also be used to imitate enamelling. The metal jewelry is made in the same way as for ordinary enamelling (see chapter 8) but the cells are filled with resin instead of enamel. However, I think resin is best used as a material in its own right, not as an imitator, and the most successful pieces of jewelry have been made using it in this way. You can take advantage of the fact that it is stronger and more resilient than enamel, and it can be used in large areas without the problems of stress and cracking.

Resin can be filed to shape, smoothed with wet and dry silicon carbide paper and then polished with rubbing-down compounds.

Perspex

Perspex is another colourful, durable acrylic material that has recently become popular with jewelry designers.

It is available in sheets of various thicknesses, and rods and tubes of many cross sections, and can be obtained in both opaque and transparent colours. It can be sawn, filed and smoothed with silicon carbide paper and polished with special perspex polishes. Pieces can be glued together with special perspex glues. The manufacturers publish booklets giving the working properties of their materials and detailing which glues and polishes should be used.

Perspex can be moulded or bent after it has been made pliable by heat, and it can be heated either by direct or indirect heat. Although a direct flame is the simplest to use, it does have certain disadvantages and you have to be very careful not to let the flame scorch the perspex as it will blister and crack very easily. Play a gentle flame over the area to be made pliable – if you only want to bend an angle, protect the rest of the perspex with asbestos. When the material softens, bend it to the required shape and hold it in

Perspex, ivory and titanium brooch. Perspex, ivory and cornelian heart earrings. Both designed by Gunilla Treen

Stones

During your experiments as a jeweller, you will at one time or another probably want to use stones, either as the major or minor part of the design. Stones have always played a traditionally important part in the history of jewelry. You will need to cultivate your chosen stone dealers, for most dealers specialize in one particular area. For instance, diamond dealers usually only deal with diamonds – the other precious and semi-precious stones are usually bracketed together, though you may find someone who is a specialist in opals or malachite. Stone dealers are usually extremely helpful and, although they are used to novices buying stones, it would at least help them if they knew the colour that you would like and the approximate amount of money that you have to spend. Do not be embarassed if you feel that the money you have is little; something can usually be found to suit your requirements.

Stones have traditionally been divided into two basic categories. The precious stones are the diamonds, rubies, emeralds and sapphires; everything else falls broadly into the category of semi-precious. Stones are available in just about every shade of colour and some are heat-treated and dyed to produce even more variations. They are also available as transparent, translucent and opaque. They can be plain or with a diversity of patterns. Many stones occur naturally in forms that are readily assimilated into a jeweller's design. Tourmaline occurs as a long lozenge-shaped crystal that is usually pink or green, or sometimes both – half of each. Stones sometimes occur as groups of naturally formed crystals which can be used in their natural state. Many modern designers have successfully used what had hitherto been regarded as purely geological

that position until it has cooled; if you do not hold it firmly, it will tend to straighten out.

An electric kiln of some kind is better for more complicated moulding. Cover the bottom of the kiln with a piece of clean soft asbestos. Place the perspex inside the kiln and leave it until it softens. When it is pliable, lift out the sheet of asbestos, slide the perspex onto the mould and press it firmly into place. Complicated shapes may need both a male and female mould to prevent the perspex from springing back.

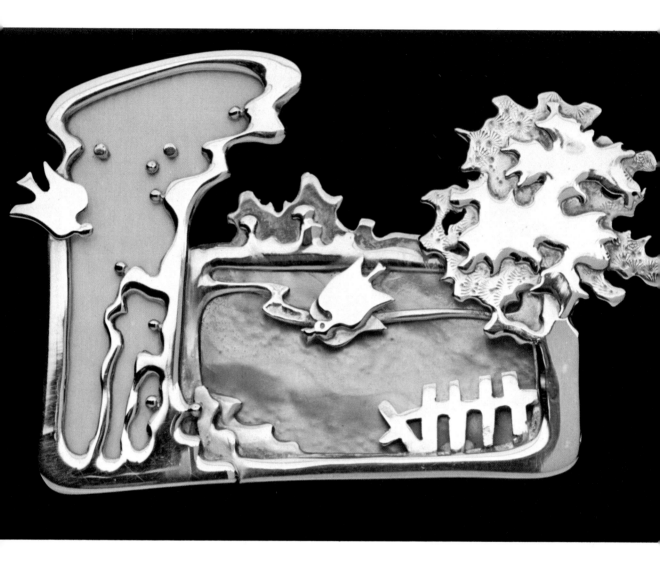

Landscape brooch in silver, 18 carat gold, ivory
and abalone shell. Designed by Patti Clarke

specimens. Tumbled stones have recently achieved a popularity with some designers. They are usually semi-precious stones of low quality which have been tumbled for several days in a machine to give them the appearance of sea-washed pebbles.

In most cases stones are cut into various shapes – faceted or *en cabochon*. Faceting is a means of introducing maximum light into the stone to emit maximum brilliance and reflection, and consequently it is usually reserved for transparent gems. If they are badly marked with inclusions they are cut *en cabochon*. Thus you can get amethysts and sapphires both faceted and *en cabochon*.

Some stones have particular qualities that can only be displayed by a specific cut. Thus 'star' rubies and sapphires are stones with other mineral inclusions, which by cutting *en cabochon* can be made to display a star on their surface.

Today it is possible to obtain a wide variety of synthetic stones – chemically made perfect crystals. For some reason there has been a feeling of 'immorality' attached to the use of synthetics but, providing no attempt is made to deceive someone that the stone is real, there is no reason why they should not be used.

There are other non-mineral sources of stones, among them pearls and corals. Pearls of many different colours and kinds can be obtained. There is the true pearl which is found naturally in the oyster in a variety of colours – white, pink, blue and black. Then there are real but misshapen pearls, known as baroque or blister pearls, which can be found in a variety of interesting shapes and colours. The supposedly inferior freshwater pearls also display interesting shapes and colours. Then again there are cultured pearls which are also real but are made by inserting a tiny perfect sphere inside the oyster, which will then

Silver, abalone shell and ivory pendant. Designed by Catherine Mannheim

proceed to cover it with layer upon layer of nacre until it resembles a real pearl.

There is a lot of traditional snobbery attached to the quality of stones, but unless you need a fine stone do not be persuaded to buy a 'better', more expensive stone unless you can see the difference. As stones vary in hardness, do not use a soft stone for something like a ring which will have to withstand hard wear and knocks. There is a scale of hardness known as Mohs scale, with diamond the hardest at 10 Mohs and talc the softest at 1, although the graduations from 1–10 are not equal. Stones registering 5 or less are unsuitable for designs in which they will be subjected to wear.

The subject of stones is such an extensive and specialized one that if you are interested in using them widely in your designs, you may like to read one of the specialist books on the subject. The following list gives a few of the more popular stones used in jewelry, with their hardness scale.

Transparent

Clear	MOHS SCALE	*Blue*	MOHS SCALE
Diamond	10	Sapphire	9
Spinel	8	Spinel	8
Zircon	$7\frac{1}{2}$	Aquamarine	$7\frac{1}{2}$
Quartz	7	*Pink*	
Green		Ruby	9
Sapphire	9	Topaz	8–9
Spinel	8	Tourmaline	7–$7\frac{1}{2}$
Emerald	8	*Yellow*	
Tourmaline	7–$7\frac{1}{2}$	Topaz	8–9
Peridot	7	Citrine	7
Purple		Beryl	$7\frac{1}{2}$
Amethyst	7	Zircon	$7\frac{1}{2}$
Red	8	*Brown*	
Ruby	9	Smoky Quartz	7
Spinel	8	Citrine	7
Garnet	$6\frac{1}{2}$–$7\frac{1}{2}$		

Translucent

Clear	MOHS SCALE
Moonstone	6
Chalcedony	7
Blue	
Star Sapphire	9
Agate	7
Green	
Agate	7
Crysophase	7
Jade	7
Red	
Star Ruby	9
Agate	7
Pink	
Rose Quartz	7
Yellow	
Agate	7
Chrysobel	$8\frac{1}{2}$

Opaque

Blue	MOHS SCALE
Lapis Lazuli	6
Turquoise	6
Labadorite	6
Green	
Agate	7
Jade	7
Malachite	4–5
Red	
Agate	7
Jasper	7
Coral	3
Brown/Yellow	
Tiger's Eye	7
Agate	7
Black	
Agate	7
Onyx	7
Haematite	$6\frac{1}{2}$
Obsidian	5
Jet	$3\frac{1}{2}$

TOOLS

Probably the most important thing is where and how you are going to sit. You will spend many hours at your workbench and it is important that you are happy and comfortable there. If you can have a properly made jeweller's bench, it should look like Fig. 1. The semi-circular cut-out enables you to sit on top of your work, and by attaching either a traditional leather skin or a piece of tightly woven canvas underneath you can catch both your filings and your work if you should drop it.

A very important and versatile piece of equipment is the bench pin (fig. 2), without which you cannot work efficiently. If you cannot have a proper bench, at least make a bench pin and clamp it to the table where you work. It has a wedge-shaped section and a large cut-out V shape. Work can be manipulated between these two prongs so that you can hold it securely. The V shape is used to support the work while you are piercing it out. By sliding the work up along the pin, even the smallest piece can be supported on both sides while the centre is pierced. If the pin is used on a jeweller's bench, a small ledge should be cut out where the pin joins the bench. This can be very useful to butt the work piece against. Never attempt to hammer on the pin as it is very springy and will give beneath the hammer blows.

Learn to use the bench pin well, it could be one of your best friends.

Another very important piece of equipment is a stool. This should be comfortable and padded, but not with plastic which will get hot and sticky. It should be a low one so that when you are sitting at the bench your shoulders should be just above the working surface. A stool that is any higher will make

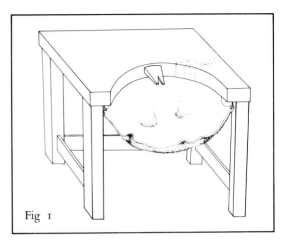

Fig 1 A traditional jeweller's workbench

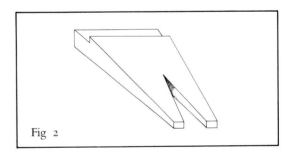

Fig 2 A wooden bench pin with V-shaped cut-out

you stoop uncomfortably over your work.

If you are going to do any heating or soldering, then you will need a large bowl of water in which to quench the work, and also an acid bath. The acid works most efficiently when hot, so it should be contained in a heat-proof glass beaker which can be kept continually warm on an asbestos mat over a flame. A slightly safer and easier method of heating the acid pickle is to use one of the small electrical fish-tank heaters used for tropical fish. A lid fitted over the beaker will prevent unpleasant fumes from escaping

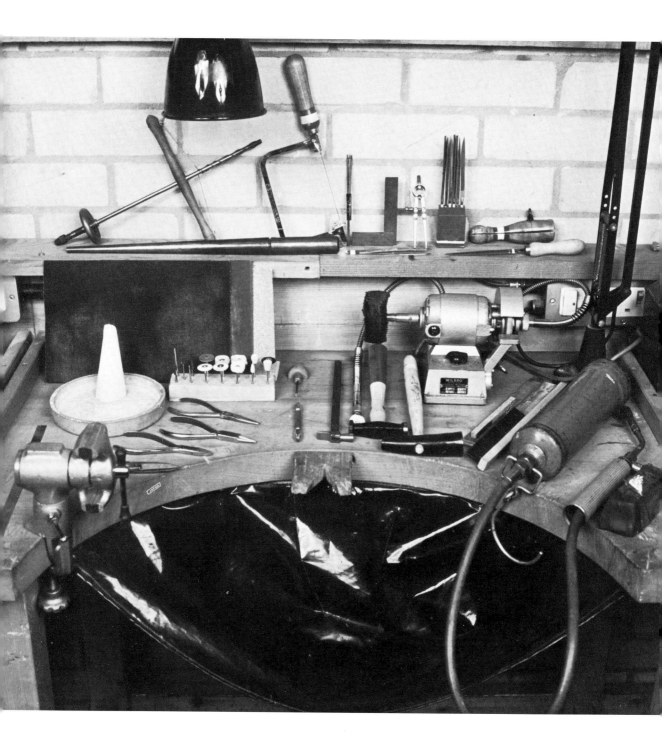

during evaporation.

The hand tools used in making jewelry have remained basically unchanged for hundreds of years. They are extremely efficient and, if used properly, will make your work easier. There is usually a 'right' way to use the tools, in which the work will progress more quickly and correctly, and this will be explained later in the relevant chapters.

Once you have gone to the expense of buying tools, take care of them and do not abuse them by using them for anything other than they were intended. Keep your tools tidy and clean – once rusted they are useless. Protect the sharp points of dividers and engravers by pushing them into corks. Try to keep files separate from each other as they will blunt their neighbours if they are continually rubbing against them. Try also to keep a separate set of files for precious and non-precious metals. The files can be kept clean with a file card.

Finally, buy the tools as you find you need them rather than spending a lot of money initially on tools you may never use.

Files

As a jeweller, the files you probably use the most are called *needle files*. These files are about 150 mm (6 in) long and the handle and the file are all one metal piece, unlike the larger files which need wooden or plastic handles fitted to them. It is also possible to buy a smaller version of the needle file, known as a *watchmaker's file*, which is very useful for getting into minute gaps. Both these types of file are available in many cross sections (fig. 3) and in two cuts, 0 and 2, 0

Jeweller's workbench with various tools of the craft

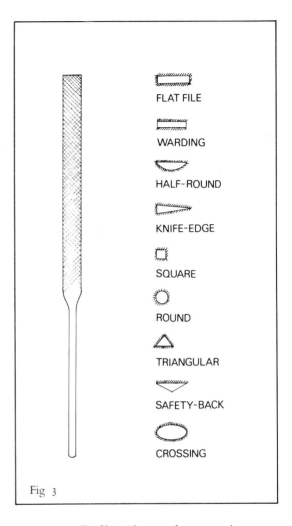

Fig 3

Fig 3 A needle file with named cross-sections

being a coarser cut than 2. There are also hand files, which have a cutting face of 150 mm (6 in), and these are commonly available as flat, round, half-round, square or triangular. Again they are available in cuts 0 and 2. You may find that some tool manufacturers give their tools different names, so if your supplier looks blank then describe the file's cross section. There are

29

times when a large 250 mm (10 in) file is needed – a half-round shape will be the most useful, giving on the one side a large flat file and on the other side a large round one, suitable among other things for the inside of ring shanks.

Rifflers are curved files which are sometimes needed to reach into awkward corners and also to file concave surfaces.

Piercing saws

Piercing saws are available plain or adjustable, enabling small portions of broken blade to be re-used. However, you may find the tedium of fiddling with scraps of blades not worth the small amount of money saved, in which case a plain saw will suffice. They are also available in different sizes and the one most suitable for jewellers has a frame depth of 100 mm (4 in) – anything larger is unwieldy. The saw blades used in these frames have teeth pointing in one direction and along one edge. They are available in a wide range of sizes from 10 to 8/0, the latter figure being the smallest. 3/0 is a fairly standard size suitable for jewellers. There are some slightly more expensive blades with rounded backs which are easier for negotiating very tight curves and are well worth the extra money.

Hammers

A *ball pein hammer* is extremely useful, and if you have one of these everyday hammers it will help you to resist the temptation to use a specialist jewelry hammer for such heavy jobs as untightening a stiff vice.

planishing hammer This is the hammer most used by jewellers. It has one round flat face and a flat square face with the edges rounded off.

collett hammer This has two softened rectangular faces and can be used for forging pieces of jewelry.

wood mallet This has a squat cylindrical head and is used for shaping metal in the initial stages without stretching it.

hide mallet This has a cylindrical head of coiled hide that has been impregnated with resin. It is also used for preliminary metal shaping.

chasing or repoussé hammer This has one small ball face and a large circular, slightly convex face. It is used for chasing and repoussé. The face of this hammer never comes into direct contact with the face of the metal – it is always used to strike another tool.

small watchmaker's hammer used for small intricate tasks.

All these hammers are available in a small range of sizes and weights.

Jewelry (and silversmithing) hammers should be kept in immaculate condition – any mark on their metal faces will be immediately implanted onto the surface of your previously blemish-free metal. Before you use a hammer check that the surface is clean, remove any marks with emery paper and then give the face a quick buff with a tripoli mop.

Pliers and cutters

The names of the pliers refer to the shape of their noses:

parallel, half-round, round, snipe nose.

wire cutters These are available with the cutting edge on the top or side.

straight jewellers' snips These are used only for cutting thin sheet and fine wire, and should not be used for cutting thick sheet, which will only strain the joint.

Vices

small engineer's vice for general use

toolmaker's vice for holding very small pieces of work

wooden ring vice for holding rings or other

pieces of work in a vice that is easy to hold and does not mark the metal
pin vice for holding fine pieces of wire and fine tools
small engineer's hand vice 50 mm × 50 mm (2 in × 2 in)

Tweezers
brass tweezers the only ones that can be used with the pickle solution
stainless steel tweezers
sprung soldering tweezers for holding or supporting pieces to be soldered together

Micrometer
This is an extremely useful though costly tool for measuring the thickness of flat sheet and wires. The metal is placed between the jaws and the screw handle tightened until it cannot be rotated any more – do not force it, you will feel immediately when the jaw has made contact. Some micrometers have a device which unlocks the screw handle when the jaws are tight enough, so that the handle keeps turning without any further tightening of the jaws. The measurement can then be read off the barrel. Micrometers are available in both metric and imperial markings – the ones with metric markings are easier to use.

Soldering torch
There is a wide variety of torches available and to a certain extent the one you choose is a matter of personal taste.
Traditionally, jewellers have used a torch where the flow of air is provided by the user blowing down the air tube. This, of course, controls the intensity of the flame and it means that very personal and intimate control can be maintained. There is a knack to using it which is easily learned and this is the type of torch that I would personally recommend for a jeweller. So if you have gas

available buy one of these small mouth-blow gas/air torches. Remember that the size of the flame is determined by the flow of gas, and the intensity of the flame by the flow of air – this applies to all torches. When you buy the torch explain whether you have 'town' gas or natural gas as they will have different modifications.

If there is no gas at hand then the next alternative is to use one of the gas/air torches for propane bottled gas. An adaptor will be needed to reduce the gas pressure but full instructions are given with the torch. Again the air is provided by blowing.

The final alternative is to buy one of the bottled gas handyman torches. With these it is not normally possible to control the air, which is drawn in automatically around the head of the nozzle. These torches are usually cheaper than the other torches mentioned and have a variety of heads that can be bought separately. However, their main disadvantage is the lack of control over the flame; although you can make it smaller or larger, it generally tends to be a small, intense flame that is not always suitable. Whichever torch you decide to buy, with continual use and practice you will learn to know your torch and become an expert with it.

Asbestos
You will need a large sheet of asbestos approximately 300 mm × 300 mm × 30 mm (12 in × 12 in × 1$\frac{1}{4}$ in) to protect the bench where you work. This should be soft asbestos, not the hard kind which can be cracked by a direct flame. Better still, in view of the health risks of using asbestos, try to get one of the man-made alternatives, especially where children are likely to come into contact with it. A small block of asbestos about 150 mm × 100 mm (6 in × 4 in) will also be useful.

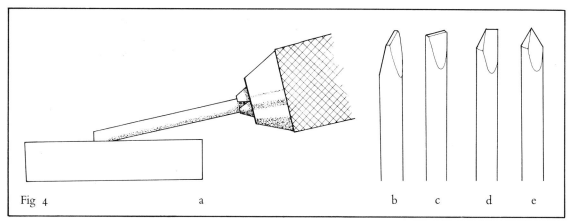

Fig 4   a   b   c   d   e

Fig 4a Needle in pin vice held in first position on the grinding stone.   b Angle of first face. c Front and back faces cut.   d Needle showing first side angle.   e Completed needle drill

Charcoal block

If you can, buy a real charcoal block. Do not be persuaded into buying a composition block, because although these are cheaper they last only a short time for they continue to burn internally after a prolonged heating operation, and when you go back all you find is a pile of grey ash. A real charcoal block can be treated to make it last even longer. Bind it tightly around its circumference with two or three strands of thick binding wire – make sure the ends are tucked safely away. Stand the charcoal block on a large sheet of asbestos and pour about $\frac{1}{8}$ litre ($\frac{1}{4}$ pint) of methylated spirits over it. Stand well back and light the block with a taper. Leave the block until the flames extinguish themselves and it is quite cool – the flames are almost invisible so do not try to pick it up unless you are sure they are really out. The flames will burn out any extraneous material in the block and the binding wire will keep the block tightly together in case it should crack.

Archimedean drill stock

This is a beautiful piece of ancient equipment used for drilling holes. You will also need a supply of fine drills, or using a needle and the following method you can make your own.

Break off the ends of the needle with a pair of pliers, taking care not to let the broken ends fly off. Hold the needle in a pin vice or a pair of pliers, at the angle shown in fig. 4a. Gently but firmly rub the needle sideways on a fine oilstone or arkansas stone, lubricated with a little oil. Continue rubbing until you have a nice 'flat', as illustrated in fig. 4b. Turn the needle over and repeat on the other side, which should leave you with a point that resembles a screwdriver (fig. 4c). Return the needle to the first position, but tilt the right side slightly sideways and upwards. Now rub a few strokes until you have a face that resembles the one in fig. 4d. This is one of the cutting angles – do not worry if the angle is not quite right first time, just try it again. Turn the needle back to the other side and repeat this. The completed needle should look like fig. 4e. Your first one may not be perfect but keep trying – it is a lot easier to do than it sounds. Henceforth you will be able to make your own drills and reshape the ones that break.

General tools

draw tongs and draw plates for making wires. The plates are available in a wide variety of sizes and shapes, the most common being round and square.

scribe a steel tool used for marking and drawing on metal

centre punch for making depressions prior to drilling holes

steel rule with metric and imperial markings

steel dividers

borax dish and cone used when soldering

paint brush (a fine child's brush will do) for painting on borax

binding wire (No. 0·3 mm)

doming block (bronze or steel)

doming punches (steel)

doming punches (wood)

steel flatting block a specially hardened block for flattening pieces of metal on, and also for checking flat edges on your work. A smallish one, about 150 mm × 82 mm × 25 mm (6 in × $3\frac{1}{4}$ in × 1 in), should suffice.

triblet for making rings you will need a steel ring triblet (sometimes called a mandrel). This is long tapered cone of hardened steel, tapering from about 30 mm to 7 mm ($1\frac{1}{4}$ in to $\frac{1}{4}$ in).

a set of ring sizes This is a set of steel rings marked with ring sizes and can be bought with or without the half sizes.

size-marked triblet This looks like a ring triblet with ring sizes marked on it. They are usually made of aluminium and are not for hammering on – only measuring.

coconut dust or cork chips in a small box 150 mm (6 in) square. This is used for drying metal.

brass bristle brush

soft and hard bristle washing-out brushes

glass fibre brush for enamelling

For finishing and polishing

Water of Ayr stones 3 mm, 6 mm and 12 mm ($\frac{1}{8}$ in, $\frac{1}{4}$ in and $\frac{1}{2}$ in) square

wet and dry silicon carbide paper grades 320, 400, 500, 600 and 800

blue-backed emery paper grades 0, 2/0, 3/0, and 4/0

plate glass a sheet large enough to take the finishing papers

emery sticks different-shaped sections of wood covered in the various grades of finishing papers

For hand polishing
hand-polishing buffs covered with fine suede, wool and felt

For machine polishing
mops 2 hard felt mops about 76 mm × 25 mm (3 in × 1 in), 2 calico mops 76 mm × 25 mm (3 in × 1 in), 1 swansdown mop 76 mm × 25 mm (3 in × 1 in), 1 soft bristle mop, 1 hard bristle mop, 1 brass bristle mop

felt ring stick

blocks of polishing compounds tripoli and rouge are the ones most commonly used, though there are specific ones available for other materials. Ask your supplier for details.

scrapers For scraping away thin slivers of metal

burnishers For burnishing a polish onto metal

Electrical tools

pendant drill This is a flexible drive attached to a motor. It has various chucks into which small drills, burrs, grinders and polishing mops can be attached. It rather resembles the old-fashioned dental drills and is worked either by a hand or foot control. It is an extremely versatile and useful tool to have.

polishing motor This is a small motor with a double-ended, tapered central spindle. The smallest you can use is $\frac{1}{2}$ h.p. – anything less powerful might be slowed down or even stopped if you leant on it heavily during polishing. It needs about 2800 r.p.m.

(If you decide to use specialist techniques such as enamelling or repoussé you will require other tools, details of which will be given in the chapter describing the technique.)

This has been a rather long, and perhaps formidable, list. You do not by any means need all of these tools but you will probably acquire most of them gradually if you take a serious interest in making jewelry. As I have already mentioned, buy the tools only as you need them. There are many other tools available too which you may one day see, buy and find invaluable—like cooks, jewellers have their own pet tools that they could not manage without.

To make your own tools

You may wish to make your own tools or to modify the tools you already have. The things that you are most likely to make are small tools, for instance those used for carving ivory or tortoiseshell. Tools are made from high-carbon steel which is then hardened and tempered. Buy a length of steel most suitable for the shape of tool that you require. If you want to forge the tool, heat it to a dull red and hammer it until you achieve the required shape. If the change of shape is extensive the steel may require several reheatings. The shape can be refined and finished by grinding and filing it.

The metal must then be hardened by heating it again to a dull red and plunging into water or a bucket of sand. It must also be tempered, as at this stage it will be brittle as well as hard. Clean the surface of the metal so that you can easily see its colour, and proceed to heat the working end of the tool until the correct colour appears.

The correct colour depends on what the tool is going to be used for. The following is a general guide:

pale yellow
220°C (428°F)   gravers, carving tools

dark yellow
240°C (464°F)   hammers, chasing tools

brown
255°C (525°F)   wood-carving tools

purple
275°C (559°F)   press tools

blue
300°C (572°F)   saw blades,
                 spring components

3
Piercing
and Filing

It is possible to make complete pieces of jewelry without heat and soldering. You simply saw the shapes, pierce them internally with designs if you wish, and then file out the irregularities.

You will have to design the jewelry bearing in mind that it is only going to be made by piercing. In other words the design will have to be flat and it will rely on its shape for interest. A pattern may be pierced out of the body of the metal using lines or areas, or a mixture of the two

There are several ways of transferring the design to the piece of metal, which should be perfectly flat and clean. The design can be drawn immediately onto the metal with a pencil and then, because the pencil will rub off as the work is handled, it must be re-outlined with a scribe, which scratches the design into the surface of the metal so that it can easily be seen. If necessary, a black wax crayon can be rubbed across the scratches, which will hold a little of the wax and show up as a black line, or the whole area of the metal may be blackened with Indian ink and the design scratched through this, when it will of course appear as a white line.

If you are not able to draw the design directly onto the metal then you must use one of the following transfer methods. Trace the design onto a piece of tracing paper and rub a pencil over the back of the paper. Rub a piece of plasticine over the surface of the

metal, which will enable the pencil lead to adhere to the metal. Place the paper, graphite side down, onto the prepared metal and retrace the design, which will be transferred to the metal underneath. Again the design must be outlined with a scribe, as explained in the previous paragraph.

Another method is to take the sheet of paper with the design on, and glue it to the metal with a paper glue or double-sided sellotape (illustration A). Using a pin, follow the outline by pricking along the design so

---

A Glue the tracing of the design onto the metal

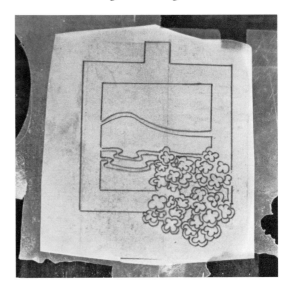

that when the paper is removed there is a series of dotted lines to follow. This is a very traditional method but one that I find very tedious, so I usually transfer my designs by the following simple method. The only time I do not recommend using this method is when the design is very geometrical, in which case it should be easy to draw directly onto the metal. Simply trace the design in ink onto tracing paper, glue the paper to the metal and then saw along the relevant lines of the drawing.

If the design is a simple shape with no interior perforations, then it is a simple matter of piercing out the shape. However if it has internal piercing, like the one in the photographs, then it will be necessary to drill holes to let the saw blade through.

TO DRILL HOLES

A centre punch must first be used to make a small depression for the drill to centre on. If this is not done the drill will wobble uncontrollably, usually badly marking the metal in the process.

Always centre punch on a steel block, never the wooden surface of a bench, because (especially if the metal is thin) it will become distorted around the mark. Place the punch on the area to be drilled and strike once with a hammer (illustration B). Place a spot of oil on the tip of the drill to aid lubrication and press the metal down on the rotating drill. If it seems to be taking a long time withdraw the drill and start again – sometimes the friction expands the metal which grips the drill. If you have a pendant drill, it is just a matter of selecting a drill slightly larger than the saw blade, placing it in the chuck and drilling the hole (illustration C). However if you have an Archimedean drill then you will have to acquire the knack of using it.

B Centre punch where holes are needed

C Drill the holes

To use an Archimedean drill

To start the drill twist the string around the vertical shaft, as illustrated (fig. 5a) – this pulls the handle up to the top of the shaft. Place your fingers on the wooden handle either side of the shaft and press firmly downwards, thus unwinding the string and turning the shaft (fig. 5b). The little weighted flywheel will continue to turn, rewinding the string which will return to its first position. Continual repetition of this process drills a hole. The technique is to press down and then allow the handle to return upwards. If you are having difficulties, check that your fingers are not touching the centre shaft as this will impede the rotation. If this is not the case, check that you are not continuing to press downwards when the handle should be on its return journey, thus preventing the string from rewinding.

The technique of using this drill takes a little time to acquire – it is rather like using a humming top – but once mastered it makes drilling holes a quick and simple process.

When using either a pendant drill or an Archimedes drill do not have more than half the drill protruding from the chuck or it will have a tendency to snap. Ensure also that the drill is held centrally in the chuck.

Now that you have made a hole, all you have to do is to learn how to pierce. If you look at the saw blade (a 3/0 blade is suitable for most jewelry) you will see that the teeth are all on one side and point downwards or upwards, depending on which way you are holding it. Now pick up the saw and hold it horizontally with the handle towards you and the frame hanging down towards your

Fig 5a Wind up the cross-handle of the Archimedes drill stock. b Press down on the handle to unwind the string and rotate the flywheel

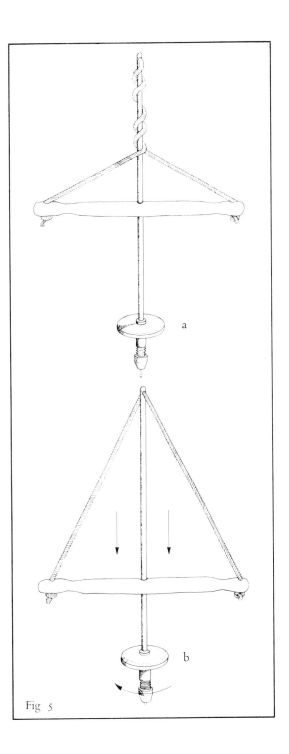

Fig 5

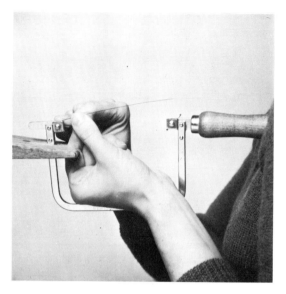

D Hold the saw frame horizontally, with the handle pressing against your body

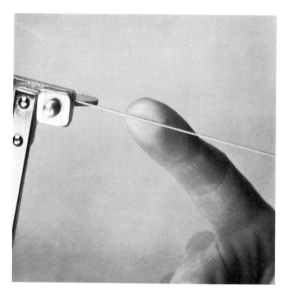

E The teeth should point upwards and towards your body

lap (illustration D). Undo the wing nuts holding the blade at each end. Now take the blade and clamp it into the end nearest to you, with the teeth facing upwards and pointing towards the handle. Check the direction of the blade by running your fingers carefully along its length (illustration E). Compress the saw between your chest and the edge of the bench and, using your free hand, clamp the other end of the blade into the frame. Release the pressure slowly or the blade may break. The blade should be taut.

The frame is now ready to use. Support the metal to be pierced on the bench pin, positioning it so that the blade will cut between the V. Hold the saw as shown in illustration F, and firmly but gently move it up and down. Use the thumbnail of your right hand as a guide to steady the blade and begin by pulling the blade down. The saw only cuts on the downward stroke, so do not push forwards

on the upward stroke. In fact it is better not to push forwards at all – the blade will make its own way forwards. Take long, even strokes – short strokes are only likely to make your line inaccurate and they are a waste of energy.

The frame should always point forwards, and changes in direction are achieved by moving the work. To turn a sharp corner or a right angle move the blade up and down slowly, but do not let the blade move forwards. At the same time quickly move the work until the blade is facing in the required direction. In actual fact you are almost drilling a hole. To pierce a curve, you will find it easier if you adopt a slightly backwards and forwards curving motion as you saw – this will prevent you from making a curve consisting of minute straights (or not so minute in some cases!).

If necessary, lubricate the blade by rubbing a small block of beeswax along it. If you have

F Move the saw firmly up and down to pierce the metal

long as the wobbles are equal on both sides, do not worry – practice will cure this. However, if you find you are continually leaning in one direction, you must consciously correct yourself. Most right-handed people find they have a tendency to veer towards the left and vice versa. Make sure that the shoulder of the arm with which you are sawing is directly behind the work, rather than to one side, and this should help.

Pierce around the outside of the pendant, as close to the line as possible, then proceed to the internal sections. To introduce the blade into the holes, undo the nut nearest the handle. Holding the saw horizontally between your chest and the bench, thread the blade through the hole and tighten the clamp with one hand, supporting the weight of the metal with your other hand. The internal sections can now be pierced out. Try to saw neatly – the smoother the edges are, the less time you will need to spend on filing.

If the pieces of metal to be pierced are very small they can be held in a small hand vice, a wooden ring clamp, or even a pair of parallel pliers. However, nothing is as sensitive as your fingers so try to hold the work – it is surprising how small a piece you can really hold if you persevere.

to stop while you are sawing, rest the metal at the bottom of the frame on top of the handle. To remove the blade from the metal either unscrew the bottom wing nut and withdraw the blade upwards, or continue to move the blade slowly up and down while pushing backwards along the line that has already been cut. If you keep breaking the blade check that it is taut, as a slack blade will drag and break. Before putting in a new blade ensure that small broken bits have not been left behind in the wing nuts.

Check also that you are holding the frame absolutely vertical in a relaxed manner, not jerking up and down and not pushing forwards too hastily. A common beginner's fault is to keep wobbling off the line but, as

FILING

Filing is most commonly used to smooth rough edges or surfaces; it can also be used to alter or refine shapes that you are displeased with. If you have anything other than a small area to remove, then go back and use the saw.

Beginners commonly think that because they are making a small piece of jewelry they must use a small file. They feel that large files are too crude and coarse, but large files can be just as smooth as small ones, depending on the cut. You should always use the largest file

39

possible in the circumstances – apart from anything else, it will save extra work. You should also use the file shape most suited to the contour being filed. Thus you would use a flat file for a straight edge, an external curve or a large internal curve. For a small internal curve use a half-round file. For sharp angles you would use a triangular or knife-edge file. Experience will show you which file is best suited to the job.

Files are designed to cut or file on the forward movement. Press down firmly and move the file forwards, allowing the file to return back without pressure. As with piercing, long smooth strokes are more efficient and accurate than short ones. The file is usually used at an angle diagonal to the work (illustration G). Hold the work firmly on the bench pin with one hand and hold the file in your other hand. Make sure you file evenly across the surface, overlapping one stroke with the next. If you examine the work, a fine diagonal pattern should be seen emerging – if the pattern is haphazard then you will know that you are not filing efficiently. Be careful when filing towards an external corner not to 'fall off' the end – this is a common beginner's tendency and will result in rounded corners.

Constantly check on what is happening – you may inadvertently be filing a slope onto what should be a right-angled face. When filing small areas, you may also be catching the file on an area you do not wish to file. For example, if you are filing an internal angle you could accidentally be filing the other side to the one you are working on, which could result in a groove. To combat this you can use a safety-back file, so called because the back of the file has no cutting edge. A pillar file also has no cutting edge on its side. If you have a fairly long straight edge to be filed, clamp the work in a bench vice

G Hold the file at a diagonal angle to the work

(making sure that the metal is protected from the vice jaws by guards made of plastic or leather) and, holding the vice horizontally in both hands, draw the width of the file towards you. This will give fine longitudinal lines and is known as draw filing.

In the piece of work illustrated, the outside edge is filed, constantly checking that the corners are right angles and that the edges are straight. A 254 mm (10 in) flat file with a fairly smooth cut would be used for this. The three internal straight sides are then filed, using a knife-edge file to reach into the corner where the flowers begin. This time it is not only necessary to check the right angles and the straight edges, the internal edges must also be parallel to the external edges. This can be done with a pair of dividers. To file around the inside of the flowers, needle files of the appropriate section should be used – in this case a half-round file would probably suffice.

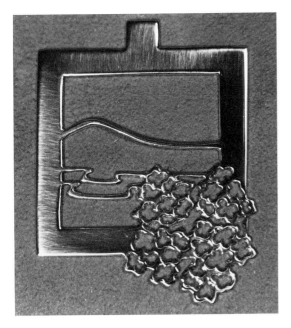

H The finished silver pendant

also abrasive discs made of various materials such as carborundum, emery and pumice.

The work illustrated has now been pierced and filed (illustration H). As it is intended to be a pendant, it will obviously need something to support a chain or necklet. In this case a small hook has been soldered onto the back, but to avoid soldering, the pendant could have been designed with a small rectangular tab protruding above the top edge – this can then be turned over with a pair of round nose pliers to make a ring for the chain to pass through. To finish and polish the pendant see chapter 9.

The work should always be supported firmly on the bench pin and manipulated so that you can work efficiently and comfortably. I have seen people trying to file in mid-air, without resting the work on a solid support – this is a waste of energy as the hand holding the work gives way under the pressure of the hand holding the file. Sometimes you will have to get into curved angles or deep concavities where an ordinary file will not reach, and here you will need to use a riffler. These are specially shaped files in almost every conceivable form. They have the cut on the internal, external, or on both faces, and are available in three sizes and several cuts.

If you have a pendant drill, there are various attachments that can be used to remove small amounts of metal. The small metal attachments are known as burrs and there are

4
Annealing
and Pickling

ANNEALING

To make jewelry that requires bending or shaping, the metal will have to be annealed. Most of the metals used in jewelry – copper, silver and gold become 'hard' as they are worked, because the crystalline structure alters as stresses and tensions are applied to the metal. Fig. 6a is a simplified diagram of the crystalline structure of silver in its soft state. The roughly circular crystals can move freely around each other. If the metal is continually hammered, the crystals become flattened and thus more immobile, making the metal harder (fig. 6b). Fig. 6c shows an uneven structure, flattened on the outside and round on the inside, the sort of structure that arises from rolling the metal to make it thinner. So it is necessary to remove these stresses and tensions which harden the metal by the process called annealing, which restores the crystalline structure to its natural flexible state. Unless the metal that you buy is known to be annealed, assume that it is not.

Annealing is the combined process of heating and cooling the metal, usually in water – do not make the common beginner's mistake of thinking that it refers only to the heating part of the process. You will need a large blue soft flame so that the metal can be heated evenly. A flame that is too small and hot will give only localized heating and may result in the metal melting. If you have the

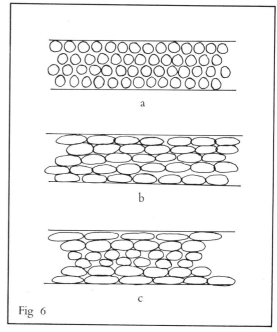

Fig 6

Fig 6a Rounded crystalline structure of soft annealed metal. b Elongated crystals formed by hammering or compression. c Unequal stress caused by rolling

flame too near to the metal, the area immediately below the flame will be left cold. Fig. 7 shows the different parts of the flame. The central bright blue cone is unburned gas. The outer edge and main body of the flame is the part we are most interested in. This is an even mixture of burning gas

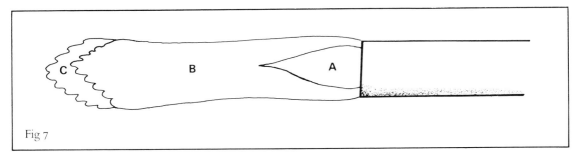

Fig 7

Fig 7 Typical flame structure used for most jewelry purposes. Section A is light blue unburnt gas. Section B is a dark blue mixture of gas and air which will be very hot – this is the section you should use. Section C is the yellow sooty tip of excess air

and air. The very tip of the flame is usually cooler and slightly smoky because it has more air mixed with it. Any flame that has too much air will tend to be yellowish and sooty, and will dirty your metal – this will be even more important when it comes to soldering.

You should support the metal on wire mesh or a soldering wig, or at least prop it against another charcoal block, so that the hot air can circulate freely underneath. If it is just laid flat on the asbestos sheet, the asbestos will tend to rob the metal of its heat, making it more difficult to heat evenly. Play the flame gently backwards and forwards over the metal, heating it evenly until it reaches a dull cherry red colour, and then quench the metal in cold water. Make sure the water covers the metal evenly – I have seen people trying to quench a 150 mm (6 in) rod of metal in 50 mm (2 in) of water!

It is quite important that the metal is heated to the correct annealing temperature. Try to anneal in a dark corner – it is difficult to see the cherry red colour in bright sunlight. If it is not possible to find a dark corner, then make a shade of a curved piece of metal

about 300 mm ($11\frac{3}{4}$ in) high and 450 mm ($17\frac{3}{4}$ in) long, which when painted black will provide enough background shade to heat against (fig. 8). Many people are concerned in case they should melt the metal. In fact the annealing temperature is considerably lower than the melting temperature, so there is a reasonable leeway.

The tensions in the metal are released gradually during the rise in temperature, and if you stop heating the metal it will still be hard. So you must continue to heat until the cherry red colour is achieved, indicating that the grains have recrystallized to give a soft metal. If you go too far and overheat you will get what is known as an 'orange-peel' surface, caused by excessive grain growth –

Fig 8 A black metal shield you could make to darken your working area

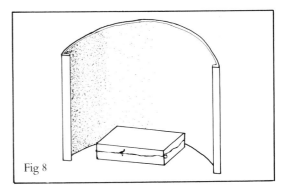

Fig 8

this makes the metal extremely brittle and hard to finish.

In most cases, this annealing process applies to gold but some carat golds require a slightly different process, for example allowing the metal to cool to black heat before quenching it. It is therefore wise to consult the manufacturers, who usually supply a booklet for workshop practice applying to their particular gold alloys.

To heat long lengths of wire, wrap them into a coil and bind the ends loosely with a small length of the same wire. If you used something like soft-iron binding wire, it would have to be removed before pickling or the pickle solution would become contaminated. Anneal very carefully to avoid melting stray ends. As the wire is heated, it may suddenly jerk and attempt to straighten itself out – these are the stresses on the wire being released.

Unfortunately, it is very easy to overheat the wire in the odd places which will make the metal brittle and cause it to crack. If you have a small kiln you can anneal the wire in the kiln, which will of course heat the metal indirectly thus preventing any possibility of overheating. Lie the coiled wire on a mesh stand and place it in a hot kiln until it reaches the required colour. Take out the stand and quench the wire in the normal way.

Another way of heating wire indirectly is to enclose it in a tin can. Take an old fruit can and heat it until the tin covering has melted and burnt off, let it cool and then rub it well with coarse emery paper until you are sure the can is clean. This is very important as any residual traces of tin will contaminate the wire. Place the wire inside the can and then heat the whole can with a very large flame.

Amber and silver chain necklace. Designed by Joan Bond

The wire inside the can will gradually become hotter and will eventually reach the annealing temperature. The wire can then be withdrawn and quenched in the normal manner.

As we have already touched on the subject of contamination, this is a convenient place to say a little more about this. If you are neat and tidy the problem will probably never arise, but always check that the area where you anneal or solder metal is clean and free from scraps of lead or left-over pieces of solder – if these are picked up by the heated metal they will eat into the surface and leave pit marks.

To heat tubing, hold the flame slightly farther away than normal. Try to heat the tube from the outside only, as the flame has a tendency to funnel and blow back if you attempt to heat the inside of the tube. This tendency can be relieved to some extent if you hold the flame at a slight angle rather than directly down the centre of the tube.

PICKLING

This is a process used to clean metal and to remove the oxides which occur on the surface of most metals after they have been heated. Most of the metals used by jewellers contain a certain amount of copper and this is the chief source of the oxide. When metals containing copper are heated, a reaction takes place between the copper and the oxygen in the atmosphere to produce copper oxide. If pure copper is heated, the oxide is easily discernible in the form of a thin flake of black, almost like charred paper, on the surface of the metal. In the case of silver, the oxide does not actually appear as a flake like copper, but forms an extra layer on the surface. In some carat golds it also forms part of the top layer of the metal, but it is hardly noticeable in the higher carat golds because there is less copper in these alloys.

Oxide discolours the metal and, because it is an impurity, may present difficulties when you come to soldering. The metal is therefore pickled in order to remove some or all of this oxide. Pickling is also used to remove the glassy residue left by some fluxes after soldering (see chapter 6). The following recipe may be used for copper, silver or gold, but use separate containers for each metal to avoid transference of the metal dissolved in the acid.

Hot solution	Cold solution
10 parts water	5 parts water
1 part sulphuric acid	1 part sulphuric acid

Some recipes also advise the addition of one part nitric acid, though I have never found that this makes any appreciable difference. Always wear rubber gloves to prepare the pickle solution and, if you have it, a rubber or plastic apron. I always wear goggles too. It's amazing how many people don't bother to wear safety clothes – it only takes five minutes to put them on and it may save you a few minutes of excruciating pain while you race for the sink or, at worst, a lifetime of misery with a scarred face.

Stand the container in the sink so that any dribbles or spillage will do no harm, and measure the water into a container. It is best to use a plastic measuring jug, in case you ever have to use hydroflouric acid which attacks glass. Prop a plastic rod in the water and dribble the measured amount of acid slowly down the rod – this is better than pouring it directly into the container as it may splash. Feel the container – it should be just warm. If it is hot, you have poured the acid in too quickly and caused excess localized heating to take place – remember

for the next time and be more careful.

The golden rule to remember is to **always add acid to water**, never the other way round as this will cause overheating and spitting and sometimes an explosion. Should you be unlucky enough to splash acid on your skin, wash immediately with running water and soap, which is an alkali and will help to neutralize the acid. The pickle solution works more efficiently when warm, so if at all possible try to heat it. You will need to put it in a heat-proof container that is not affected by the acid – heat-proof glass is usually best. Place the container on an asbestos mat and then heat it over a bunsen flame, or on an electric ring. A very cheap and efficient method is to use one of the aquarium heaters used for tropical fish, which can be used with a thermostat to control the heat.

For a 'safe' pickle you can use powdered alum and water, 55 g (2 oz) alum to $\frac{1}{4}$ litre ($\frac{1}{2}$ pint) water. However, this is very slow and not as satisfactory as the recipes given above. If you are using alum rather than acid, then the pickle must definitely be used hot. As the water evaporates the level must be topped up. If the work is not too small you can pick it up in brass or nickel tongs and place it in the acid bath. *Never* use iron tweezers or tongs as they will contaminate the acid and cause everything placed in it afterwards to have a pink coating of iron oxide. If the work is very small, it should be attached to a length of the same wire as the work and then dangled in the pickle. Generally the work should be left in for about 1 minute, by which time the oxides on the surface will have dissolved and in the case of silver the surface will have a beautiful matt white finish. Rinse the metal in clean water and either dry on an old rag or in a box of cork dust. Some people quench the metal immediately

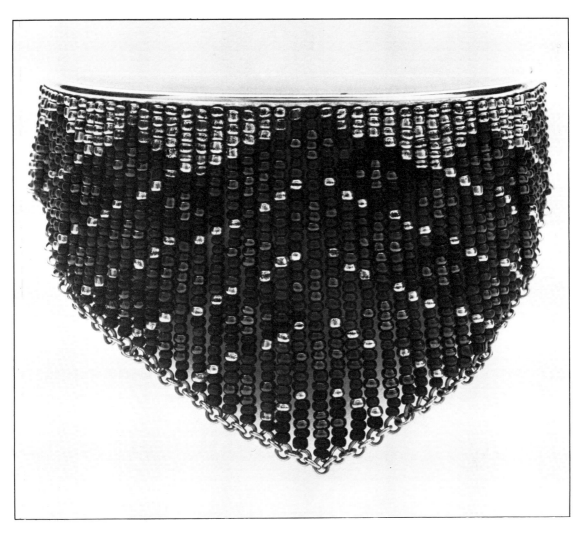

Collar of coloured beads on silver wire. Designed by Beatrice Liaskowski

in the pickle solution rather than the water, but this is not a method that I advocate – for two reasons. Firstly it is dangerous – the hot metal causes the acid to spit and give off noxious fumes – and secondly it impairs the surface of the metal – when the metal is very hot the crystalline structure is open, but on contact with the cooler pickle the structure contracts, entrapping minute particles of acid in the surface layer which may begin to eat into the metal. Continuous use of this practice leaves the surface of the metal pitted. When the piece of work is finished, just prior to polishing, it may be left in the hot pickle solution for about 10 minutes, which will leave a thick layer of the purer metal on the surface.

5
Bending
and Shaping

Silver, gold and copper are so malleable that they can be coaxed into many different shapes by means of bending, hammering and stretching. A bar of silver can be hammered to give a variety of thicknesses and shapes. A wire can be twisted into intricate patterns depending upon its thickness, and a sheet can be bent into many shapes. It is useful to know the inherent qualities of the metals that you are using and there are many exercises that you can undertake to give some indication of these qualities. Metal that is going to be shaped or bent should be in its softest form, i.e. freshly annealed and pickled.

One of the exercises to show the qualities of metal is a simple angle-bending exercise. Take a piece of flat sheet and clamp it in a vice (with the jaws protected). Then take a block of flat wood and place it with its largest face touching the half of the metal protruding from the vice. Using your hands, press the wood against the silver down towards the vice until you have made an angle of about 120° – examine the metal and you will see that the corner has a pleasant soft radius (fig. 9a). Replace the wood and press down again until you have an angle of about 90°, when you have a right angle with a soft radius – this is the natural curve of that

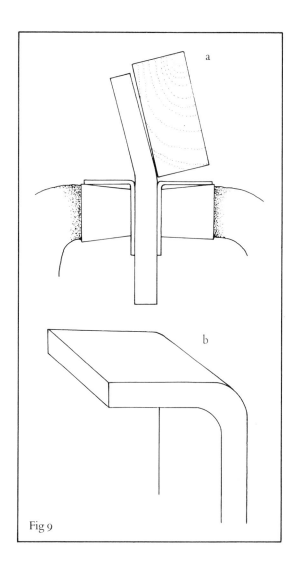

Fig 9a Bend the sheet of metal with a wooden block. b This type of soft-radius angle is produced by following fig 9a

48

thickness of metal and, as such, has a pleasing quality that can be exploited (fig. 9b). If you wish, you can use a planishing hammer and by continually hammering back and forth along the edge of the metal in the vice the soft radius can be diminished and a harder angle achieved. To make an extremely sharp right angle, a sliver of metal has to be removed from the inside edges of the angle (fig. 10a). By using either a square file or a scoring tool, a 90° angle of silver can be removed from the inclusive angle, so that when the two sides are folded up the edges of the V touch to give a sharp right angle (fig. 10b). Other-sized angles can be made by removing the appropriate amount of metal from the inclusive angle. To ensure that the angle is really sharp, the groove must extend at least seven-eighths of the way through the thickness of the metal, leaving only enough to hold one side to the other. After the angle has been bent satisfactorily, solder should be run along the join. A file is adequate for angles of 30 mm ($1\frac{1}{4}$ in) in length or less, but for longer lengths you should use a scorer. A scorer is a sharpened angle of metal that removes a sliver of metal as it is pulled towards the user. The action is repeated to make the groove the required depth. A length of straight wood can be used to guide the scorer as it cuts the groove.

To give metal soft curves, it can be hammered over shaped mandrels. The mandrel should be as near as possible to the shape and size of the curve that is required. To simply change the shape of the metal, use a wood or hide mallet – this will shape the metal without altering its thickness in any way. However, some shapes are so acute that the thickness of the metal will have to be altered to accommodate the change. Therefore, to stretch and thereby thin the metal you will need a metal hammer. If the

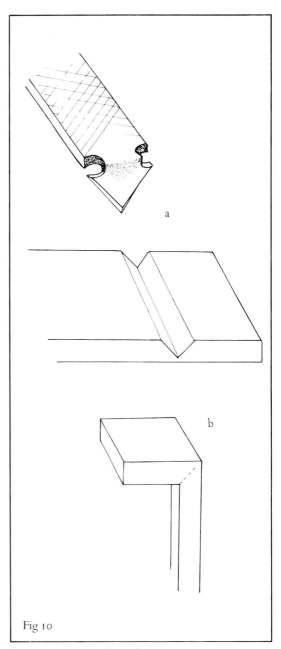

Fig 10

Fig 10a A sheet of metal with an angle cut by a scoring tool. b The right angle bent up and soldered

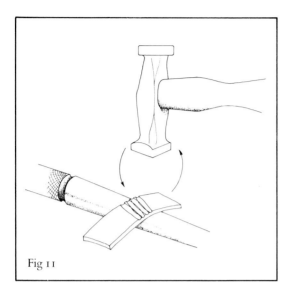

Fig 11 The planishing hammer should follow a circular motion when you are striking the metal

metal is compressed between a steel stake and a steel hammer it will become thinner. Hold a planishing hammer as in fig. 11 and stand with the arm holding the hammer directly behind the work, so that an imaginary line can be drawn up through the work, along the hammer handle and up your arm – this is very important and is the most efficient and accurate way to work. Keep your wrist fairly stiff so that the action of hammering comes from your shoulder rather than your hand. Do not strike the metal directly up and down as if driving in a nail; the hammer head should move sideways away from the work after the blow has been administered, so that the action is almost circular. Once established, you will find this rhythm is comfortable and enables you to hammer with less fatigue. Each hammer stroke should overlap the next so that the metal is stretched or bent evenly – if the hammering is

haphazard it will create a badly marked surface that is difficult to finish evenly, and curves will tend to be a series of small flats rather than an even smooth shape.

To help you understand more about bending, we will make the ring in fig. 12a. This ring will be made without soldering, and you can see that the split that will be necessary in this design has been incorporated as a feature of the design. Rings are sometimes made with a split so that the finished ring will fit several finger sizes easily. Normally they have a rather uncompromising split to be worn at the back of the finger, but this is rather an unsatisfactory answer to what is essentially a design problem – how to design a ring that will encircle the finger without being joined by soldering. There are numerous ways to solve this problem and fig. 12a is just one of them.

In this case, the ends of the ring are flower forms and when the ring is worn the two flowers with the split between them are on the front of the finger. Fig. 12b shows the ring drawn in its unbent form as a flat sheet. Following the procedure outlined in chapter 3 the design should be transferred to a sheet of metal, pierced out and filed smooth. As the metal is now to be bent into a ring, it should be annealed to make it malleable. Then the metal must be pickled clean, otherwise the layer of oxide would be pressed onto the surface of the metal when it is hammered. We will use a hide hammer, because we only want to shape the metal and not stretch it. If you are right-handed hold the hammer in your right hand, take one end of the metal firmly in your thumb and fingers and place the other end on a tapered ring mandrel with about 6 mm ($\frac{1}{4}$ in) protruding over the centre point. The object is to push the metal across the small air gap onto the curved surface of the mandrel. You

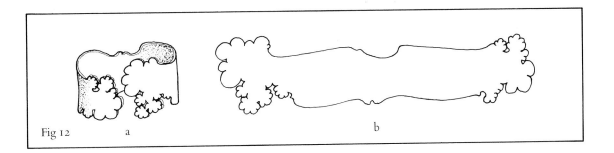

Fig 12   a   b

Fig 12a A pierced ring.   b Flat drawing of the ring extended

will hear if you make contact correctly because the metal will give a resounding ring when struck with the hammer – if you fail to make contact you will hear a dull clunk, and this sound will be even more pronounced if you use a metal hammer.

Continue hammering, at the same time feeding the metal across the mandrel, remembering to overlap each hammer stroke until you reach half-way. Turn the metal around and this time hold the curved part in your fingers and start from the straight end. It is easier to curve both ends of the metal this way – if you were to continue straight from one end to the other you would find it very difficult to both hold and curve the last part, as the ring will now be much harder and will spring every time it is struck with the hammer. Check that an imaginary centre line running horizontally around the ring is level – it is very easy to make one side slightly higher than the other. If the ring is not a true circle, replace it on the mandrel and, holding it underneath, hammer evenly around the ring again until a true circle is achieved. Each time one complete circumference is completed, take the ring off the mandrel and replace it from the other side. This will correct any slight tendency you may have to

make it conical. The ring must never be pushed so far up the mandrel that it is a tight fit – you should always work on the area of the mandrel just below the place where it fits tightly, or again the ring will become conical as the top edge will stretch where it fits tightly.

A quick check to see if the ring is a true circle is to look at the inside of the ring, which should be completely shiny. The action of hammering bruises the interior surface of the ring as it makes contact with the mandrel, and if there are any matt gaps this will indicate that the circle is still not true. Check the ring size – if it is correct all well and good. If it is too large the normal procedure is to take out a sliver of metal along the original solder seam, but as this ring has no joint the shapes at the front will have to be refiled, taking away enough metal to close up the gap and thereby reducing the ring to its correct size. If the ring is too small, then it will have to be stretched at the back. This is done with a metal planishing hammer which, if you remember, will compress the metal, making it thinner and larger. Place the ring back on the mandrel and hammer just the back half of the ring following the procedure already outlined. You will notice that the hammer makes facets on the surface – this is because the hammer face is flat and thus the metal will be squeezed out at the edges of the

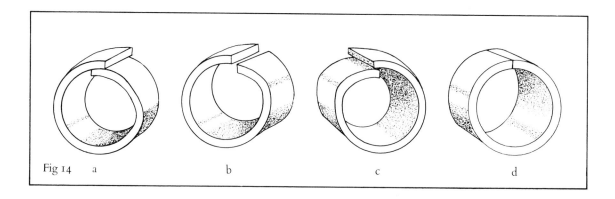

Fig 14   a   b   c   d

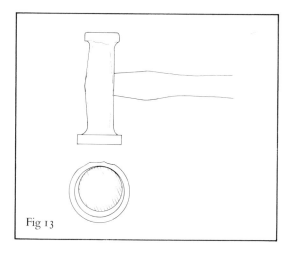

Fig 13

Fig 13 A planishing hammer thinning and thereby stretching a ring on a ring mandrel

Fig 14a Push the right side under the left side. b Pull the right side back to the opening. c Push the left side under the right side. d Pull apart and let go. The two sides should now be springy, and by a little manipulation you can make them fit

hammer (fig. 13). As long as you remember to overlap each hammer stroke carefully, then the resulting finish should be a fairly smooth curve composed of many tiny facets, which can then be filed away with a smooth hand file. The ring can then be finished as outlined in chapter 9.

Although the procedure that has just been described is for a split ring, the method of shaping is exactly the same for a ring that is going to have a soldered seam. The ring does not have to be perfectly round to be soldered. The most important thing is that the two edges to be soldered together meet perfectly to make a good joint. The ring can then be made round after it has been soldered.

To make the edges to be soldered meet perfectly, make the ring springy by pushing first one edge and then the other under the face of the opposite edge (fig. 14a). Press downwards on one of the edges and push it under the opposite face, pull this edge back and you will find it is springy (fig. 14b). Do the same to the opposite edge (fig. 14c). The two edges should now be pressing firmly against each other (fig. 14d). If the join is not perfectly straight, saw through it with a piercing saw – the blade will saw off any protruberance, thus allowing the two edges to meet better. This can be repeated until a perfect join is achieved.

Silver armband. Designed by Pierre Degan

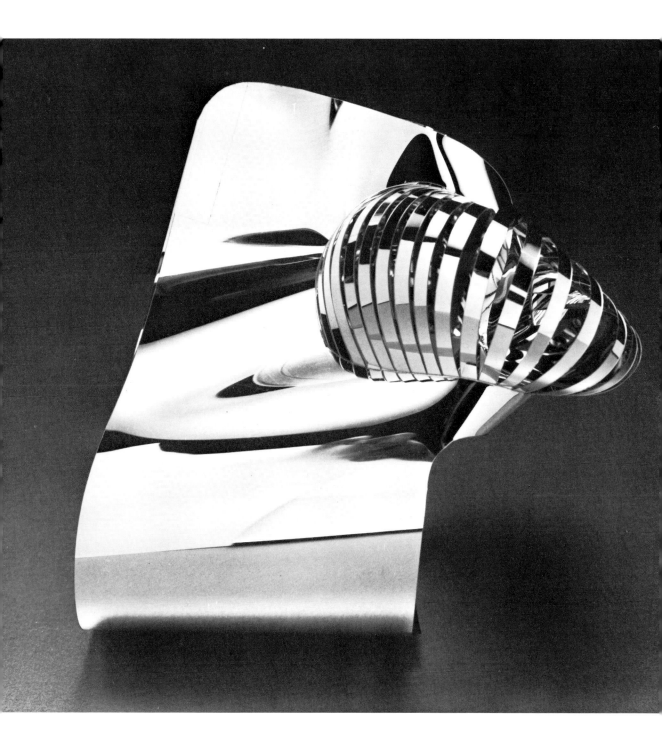

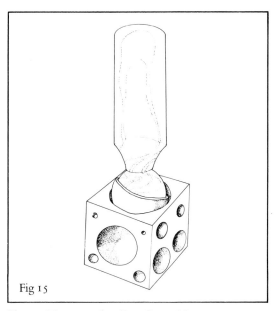

Fig 15 Hammer the disc of metal between a doming punch and doming block, rotating the metal continually

size, hammer the metal down into the recess. Rotate the metal backwards and forwards within the recess so that all parts of the metal are struck between the doming block and punch (fig. 15). It is necessary to do this to achieve a uniform curve, otherwise the metal will have a domed base with straightish sides (figs. 16a, 16b). Proceed from larger to smaller concavities, using correspondingly

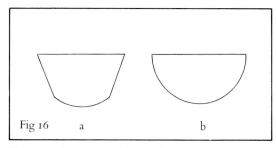

Fig 16a The wrong shape achieved by insufficient doming of the sides. b The correct domed shape

The method outlined for bending a ring can basically be applied to any curve through one plane that you would like to make. To make larger or smaller curves, the metal would be hammered over the appropriate-sized mandrel, e.g. a bracelet shape would be hammered over a bracelet mandrel. Always use a mandrel that is slightly smaller than the finished curve that you require, as the metal will always spring back slightly.

To make a shape that is a dome or part of a dome, you would use a doming block and punch. Cut out the outline shape that you require, remembering that the finished diameter will reduce during doming. As usual, the metal should be annealed and pickled. Place the metal in the largest concavity on the doming block, whatever the final required size is. Then, using a metal or wooden doming punch of a corresponding

smaller punches until you reach the required size. If you attempt to make a small dome immediately, you will in all probability split and crease the metal because it cannot accommodate a drastic change in shape in one action. Remember to choose a punch that will leave enough space between it and the doming block for the thickness of the metal, or all three will jam together. Like steel hammers, a steel doming punch will stretch and thin the metal more than a wooden one. If a very large dome is required – at least as large as the largest one in the doming block – you will need to start the doming off on a sandbag. First hammer a recess into the centre of the bag with the largest doming punch, then proceed to use it as if it were a doming block.

Small, thin pieces of metal may be bent and shaped with pliers. The technique is not to

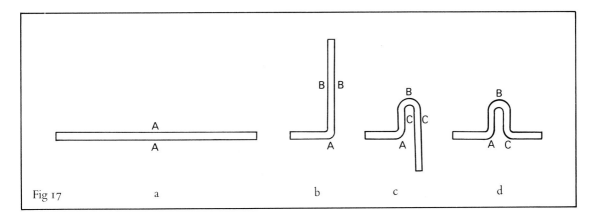

Fig 17   a   b   c   d

Fig 17   An exercise to bend wire with round nose
pliers

achieve the change in shape by just squeezing
the metal between the two jaws of the pliers,
but rather to use the jaws as a kind of
mandrel. Round nose pliers are used for
small tight bends or circles (fig. 17a). The
following is an exercise to demonstrate how
the pliers are used. First, gently but firmly
hold the annealed wire or sheet at point A
with the wire horizontal to your body. Twist
the wire backwards away from your body
(fig. 17b). Now hold the wire at point B and
twist the wire forwards (fig. 17c). Grip the
wire at point C and twist backwards – by
now you should have a piece of wire that
resembles fig. 17d. Remember not to squeeze
the wire which will only dent it. Half-round
pliers are used for larger curves, with the
curved face against the side of the metal to be
turned in and the flat side on the outside so as
not to mark the metal (fig. 18). The pliers are
very useful for bending up ring shanks, as an
alternative to hammering on a mandrel. Flat
pliers can be used to bend angles – always
place the jaws of the pliers just in front of the
line where the internal angle should

come. Parallel pliers whose jaws open in a
parallel rather than in a pivot action are very
useful for holding tiny articles, such as
brooch hinges, while you work on them.
Some pliers have a small triangular groove
ground into one side, which enables you to
hold very fine wires.

The doming or stamping principle can also
be used to make more complicated shapes,
particularly if you have access to a fly press.
In industry this method is used to produce
many of the silver articles we see on sale
today. However for the purpose of the
jeweller who is usually making only one or
two of the same article, such expense is not
justified, but the principle for stamping by
hand is just the same. It consists basically of
compressing a piece of metal between a male
and female form, for example if you wanted

Fig 18   Cross-section of half-round pliers being
used to bend up a ring shank

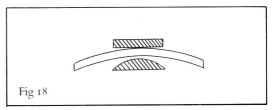

Fig 18

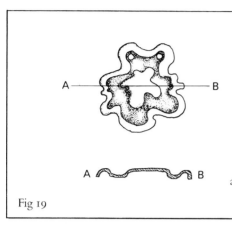

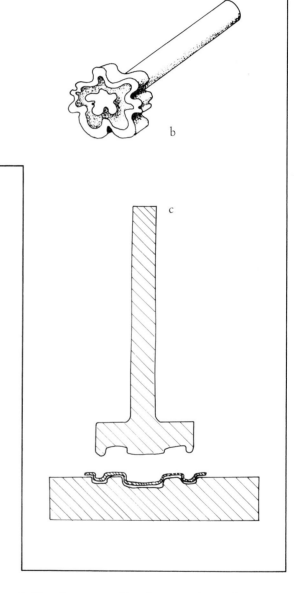

Fig 19

Fig 19a Front and cross-section of stamped necklace component.

to make several discs (as in fig. 19a) as the components for a necklace.

First the male component A would be made. This should be made from brass or mild steel, filed and ground until the correct shape is achieved. The surface of the metal head should be made smooth and polished, otherwise any small imperfections would be transferred to the silver. When the head is finished, solder it to a rod about 20 mm ($\frac{3}{4}$ in) in diameter and long enough to be held comfortably – about 150 mm (6 in) (fig. 19b). Using a heavy hammer, drive the tool into a block of lead. You may have to repeat this action several times until the correct depth is reached, making sure each time that you realign the shaped head with the recess before striking with the hammer. Eventually an exact female replica of the male head will be formed. Lay a sheet of thin annealed silver, about 8 B.M.G., across the hollow in the lead block and strike it with the male stamp (fig. 19c). If you do it accurately, the shape should be formed with one blow. If not, you will have to repeat the action until the shape is correct. Emery the surface of the

b Female stamp soldered onto rod.   c Cross-section showing thin metal compressed between male and female moulds

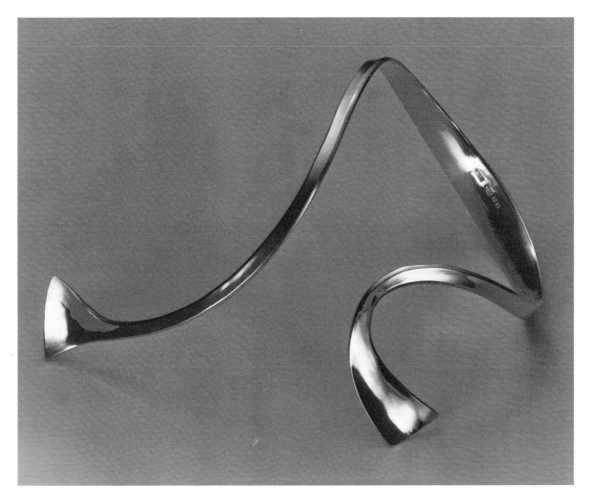

Silver forged necklet. Designed by Eric Clements

silver to remove any flakes of lead that might have adhered to the surface, which would eat into the silver on subsequent heating. Using this principle, it is quite easy to make even fairly complicated shapes.

The lead block should always be remelted before you use it again, as continual hammering compresses the block and makes it difficult to use. To remelt or make the first lead block, put the lead into a smelting ladle or an old large saucepan and either heat it from beneath with a large flame or place it in a furnace. While the lead is melting, press a tin or block of wood into a bucket of sand to make a depression equal to the size of the lead block required. Pour the molten lead carefully into the depression and allow it to cool. When it is cold, scrape away the surrounding sand and trim any thin slivers of escaped metal, known as 'flash', off the lead block. Try not to melt lead in a confined space as the fumes can be toxic.

6
Soldering

Soldering is a method of joining two pieces of metal together permanently and invisibly. The soldered joint should be as strong as the rest of the metal and should in fact make two pieces of metal one.

Copper, silver and gold, the three main metals used in jewelry, can all be soldered. The solder is usually composed of the metal concerned, plus some other metal that has a lower melting temperature thus causing the solder to melt before the metal to be joined. In the case of hard silver solders (those suitable for soldering silver, copper, iron, etc.), the solder is composed mainly of silver with the addition of zinc – the zinc being the metal required to reduce the melting point.

Solders usually come is varying degrees of hardness – the harder they are, the higher the temperature at which they melt and the less zinc they contain. Silver and gold solders come in four grades: enamelling, hard, medium and easy. A silver solder called 'easy-flo' is also available for use on copper, but it should not be used on silver as it does not always pass the assaying test for purity. Gold solders also come in varying colours, so that they can be matched to the metal they are to be used for, i.e. to solder 18 carat red gold you would use 18 carat red gold solder. In the case of gold solders, it is acceptable to use higher carat solders on lower carat golds, but not vice versa. If you are soldering small amounts of gold onto silver, use gold solder.

Until you are accomplished at soldering, you will very likely get the smaller parts hot first and, as solder flows towards the hottest part, it may flood over the smaller (in this case, gold) components. It is therefore best if the gold is flooded with a solder that is near its own colour.

Solder can be bought in strips or sheets. Gold solders come in very thin squares, already stamped with their grade. Mark your silver solders with an initial that will immediately signify what each is, e.g. N – enamelling, H – hard, M – medium and E – easy. When you are using the solder, make sure that any remaining pieces have the initial still left on them or you may make costly mistakes. Keep the solder separately from silver as it is very difficult to distinguish between them.

The reason why there are various grades of solder is so that during complex soldering operations the first pieces soldered on do not fall off while you are soldering the last pieces. Thus you would use hard solder for the first joints, then medium and then easy. Enamelling solder is very rarely used unless absolutely necessary, as its melting temperature is very close to the melting temperature of silver. During the soldering operation the zinc content in the solder will

Silver, 18 carat gold and pearl necklace. Designed by Gerda Flockinger

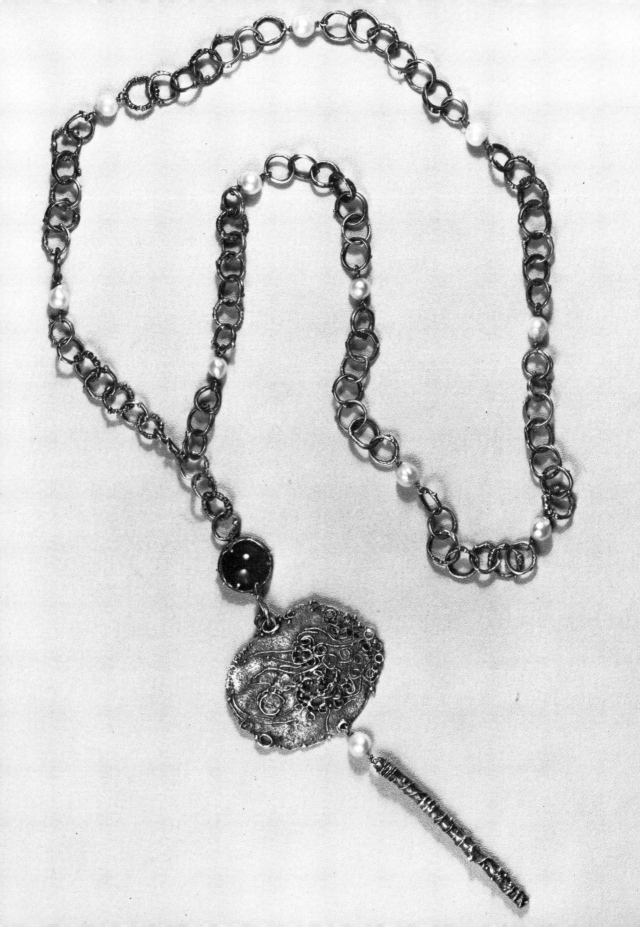

Silver, ivory and 18 carat gold pendant. Designed by Patti Clarke

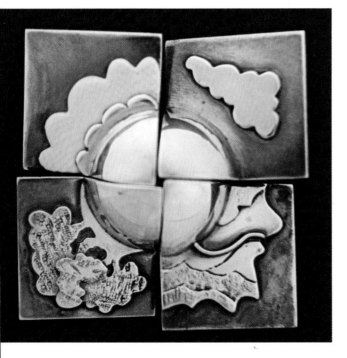

Silver, gold and ivory brooch. Designed by Catherine Mannheim

partially burn out, leaving behind a solder with a much lower zinc content which will therefore not remelt as easily. When you become more expert at soldering and can judge the melting temperatures accurately, you will find you only need to use one solder. In that case use hard solder, as it will appear less yellow on the finished piece of work than the lower-melting-point solders.

To solder most metals, including gold, silver and copper, a flux must be used on the parts to be soldered. During heating the flux forms a glassy protective surface which inhibits oxides from forming on the surface of the metal, keeps the surface clean and also encourages the solder to run. Flux is commonly available in three forms: a solid cone, a powder and a liquid. There are also special preparations of flux suitable for particular solders, for example some are specially for use with low-melting-temperature solders, so when buying flux ensure that it is suitable for the work intended. Some manufacturers also supply their own prepared fluxes which are often very good. A popular flux is common borax which comes in a solid cone. The borax is ground with water to a thin paste the consistency of milk, using a borax dish which is usually made of coarse stoneware. Use the cone and dish like a pestle and mortar. Grind only enough for the job in hand as the borax very quickly thickens and collects in a dirty crust round the edge of the dish. As any dirt is an inhibitor to good soldering, it makes sense to keep the borax clean.

There is also a commercially prepared vivid green flux that is suitable for jewelry. As it is a thin liquid it does not bubble as thickly during heating as common borax, which can sometimes be a little bulky and obtrusive when soldering tiny pieces together. However, its very liquidity can be a

disadvantage during prolonged soldering operations as it tends to burn away and no longer protects the areas to be soldered. As a novice to soldering, begin by using borax but when you have gained more experience it is probably advantageous to use a liquid flux.

PREPARATION OF WORK

The procedures outlined below are those used for soldering silver, but they also apply on the whole to copper and gold as well. Where there is a major difference in the procedure, details are given separately.

Silver pendant with garnets. Designed by Sally Day

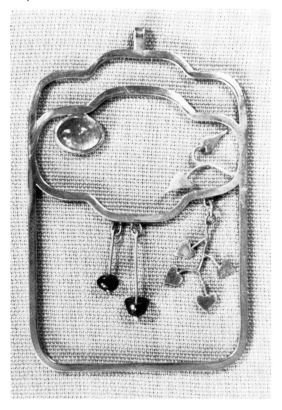

One of the most important aspects of soldering is the preparation of the work to be soldered. Time spent now on preparing and cleaning the work will make the soldering process easier and mean that less time will have to be spent cleaning up afterwards. As far as jewelry is concerned, the two components to be joined should be in as finished a state as possible. Surfaces intended to be smooth should be free of scratches and have the final fine, emery-smooth finish (see chapter 9). In some cases the pieces can even be polished, for it is sometimes very difficult to polish right into the tight angles that may be formed by soldering two pieces together. Heating during soldering should not destroy the high finish of the work – it will certainly dull the finish, but a quick buff on a soft mop should restore this. Obviously some pieces of work cannot be finished to any degree until the soldering has been finished (for example, the first soldering on a ring shank). The degree of finish must therefore be made relative to each piece of work, but the general rule is to finish the pieces to be joined as far as possible. The two edges that are to be soldered together should fit perfectly – solder is not designed to be used as a gap filler and if they do not fit the joint will be weak and look untidy. Not only that, it shows a shoddy attitude towards good craftsmanship.

The edges should also be free of any dirt or grease, as should any of the tweezers, flux, solder, etc. that you will be using. Dirt and grease inhibit solder from flowing freely. If the work has been polished, wash it well in a solution of ammonia, detergent and water to degrease it. Carefully refile the edges to be jointed so that the fresh bare metal is exposed. Paint the two edges carefully with a thin solution of flux – do not flood the flux haphazardly all over the work, for the purpose of the flux is to encourage the solder to run

and it should only be painted where the solder is to run.

If the joints can be assembled by merely laying one piece on top of or next to another, then assemble the pieces on an asbestos pad or charcoal block. Heavy or bulky pieces should be laid on a fine stainless steel mesh trivet which will lift the body of the work slightly away from the asbestos, thus enabling the heat to circulate underneath. Some pieces will not readily lie next to each other and may require a little ingenuity to hold them together. If you have a tray of carborundum chips, you could use this to support the work. Press the pieces of work into the chips arranging the edges to be soldered well above the chips. This will hold even the tiniest pieces of wire. The pieces can also be propped up and wedged together with supports of wet asbestos – this should be gently dried before soldering, or the asbestos will take away too much of the heat and prolong the soldering. Pieces of wire can also be held together by pushing them into a charcoal block which is quite soft and should hold them quite secure. This method can only be used for a simple construction.

For more complex soldering operations, there is a commercial preparation available on the market today which looks rather like a mixture of plasticine and white clay. It is very malleable and can thus be moulded to hold together the various components to be soldered. During the soldering the heat dries out and hardens the preparation, which can then be easily crumbled off.

Another method similar to this, and one which has been used with extremely good results, is suitable when a considerable number of small components have to be soldered together. Push the units to be soldered into a bed of plasticine in the required arrangement. Then make a low wall of plasticine to surround the work – just higher than the

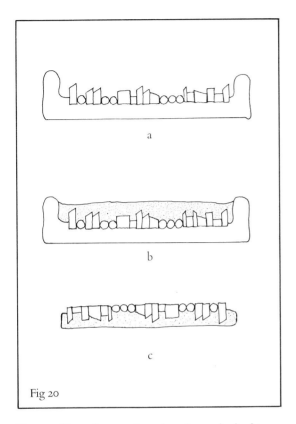

a

b

c

Fig 20

Fig 20a Press the metal sections into a bed of plasticine. Surround them with a low wall of plasticine.   b Pour plaster into the mould and leave to set.   c Peel away the plasticine to expose the backs of the metal sections, ready to be soldered together

tallest component (fig. 20a). Mix up a thick solution of plaster of paris, or investment plaster, and pour it into the mould over the work (fig. 20b). When the plaster has set, carefully peel away the plasticine wall and bed to expose the backs of all the components. Scrape away any of the plaster covering the metal, and also any plaster in the way of the areas to be soldered. The pieces can now be fluxed and soldered in the normal way, the plaster holding the work securely (fig. 20c).

Try to keep the plaster to a minimum or the whole job will require a considerable amount of time to heat up.

You can also make supporting frame works, or 'jigs', of copper or steel to hold the work, but remember not to make the jig too bulky or it will rob the work of its necessary heat.

Soft iron binding wire can be used to bind work together. It is more commonly used by silversmiths who have to hold large pieces of work together. The wire comes in varying thicknesses and you should choose the size most suitable for your work. As before, the areas to be soldered must fit correctly – do not try to use the wire to pull two faces together by force, this will only result in deep scars in the surface of the metal. The wire is used just to secure the two pieces (fig. 21). Do not allow the solder to come into contact with the

Fig 21 Secure the cufflink back and front together with binding wire

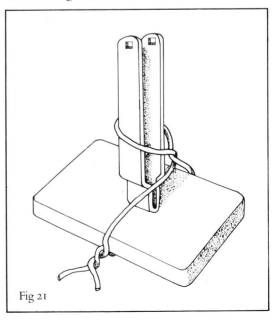

Fig 21

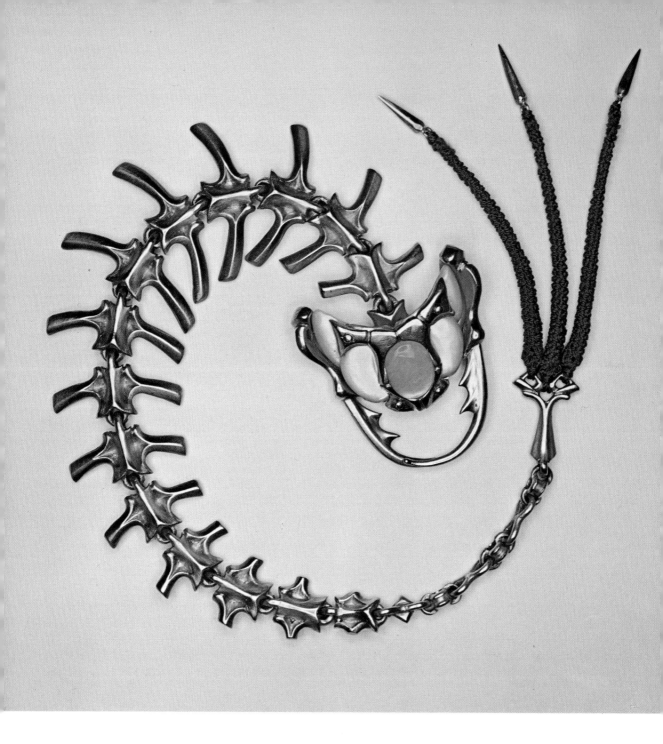

Snake bracelet, one of two designed by David
Courts and Bill Hackett. Centrifugally cast in 18
carat gold. The jaws, of 18 carat white gold and
set with mother of pearl, lock into the tail to
which are attached woven silk tassles

64

wire or it may be soldered to the work – this will be more of a problem if you are in the habit of using too much solder. As soon as the work has been soldered, snip the wires to prevent them biting into the metal as they cool. Never pickle work that still has binding wire attached to it, as the iron will contaminate the acid and cause everything put into the pickle to be coated with a layer of red iron oxide.

These are just a few of the ways in which work can be held together – a modicum of ingenuity should provide many more.

Now the work is ready for the solder to be applied. In jewelry, solder is applied most commonly in the form of paillons, which are little snippets of solder. The solder should be made very thin either by hammering or by putting it through a rolling mill to about 0·25 mm. Emery the solder until it looks bright, then cut it with jeweller's snips (fig. 22). To prevent the solder from flying everywhere, put your middle finger behind the solder as you cut, or cut into a piece of paper.

Pick up the paillons of solder with the flux brush and place them along the joint, if

possible touching both of the sides to be soldered. By picking up the paillons with the flux brush, they also become coated with flux at the same time. Alternatively, you can pick them up with tweezers, dip them in the flux and then place them on the joint. If one side of the joint to be soldered will never be seen, place the solder there – for instance, on the inside of a bezel. Otherwise place the solder on the side most accessible for cleaning it afterwards. Experience will teach you how much solder to apply, but it is better to use a small amount which can be added to if necessary, rather than too much which will take you valuable time to clean away afterwards.

When the solder has been placed in position, begin to heat the work *very gently* to evaporate the water from the flux – if you heat it too aggressively, the water will boil out madly and the paillons of solder will be flung off. As the work is heated, the flux will rise and gently bubble, but as you continue to heat it the bubbles will subside and the flux will take on a glassy appearance. If the solder has moved, push it back at this stage with an old saw blade or a piece of iron binding wire. The large gentle flame that you should have been using can now be made hotter as you concentrate on bringing the metal up to the required soldering temperature. To make an effective joint, the two pieces to be soldered must reach the same temperature together, so when soldering a small piece to a large piece always heat the large area first; the small piece will become hot indirectly and it will only be necessary to concentrate the heat on it at the last minute. As you continue to heat the metal, watch the paillons of solder and gradually you will see them begin to melt. At this stage, point the flame directly onto the joint to be soldered and the solder should now begin to flow readily. Pass the

Fig 22 Mark solder clearly and cut off paillons as you need them

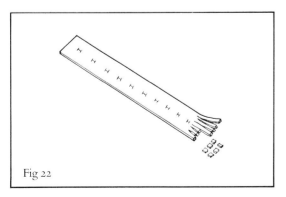

Fig 22

flame backwards and forwards along the length of the joint, heating both sides of the metal. The solder always flows towards the source of heat, so this will encourage the formation of a good joint. The molten solder will also be drawn along the joint by capillary action. When the soldering is complete, allow the work to cool slightly and then quench it in water. Check the joint and, if it is not adequately soldered, reflux it and add more solder. If the soldering has been completed satisfactorily, pickle the metal to remove the glassy flux. The work can then be finished as described in chapter 9.

SWEAT SOLDERING

This method of soldering is used when two flat pieces are to be joined face to face, and it would be too difficult or tedious to place enough paillons of solder along the edges of the pieces to solder them together adequately.

Flux completely one of the two faces to be soldered, and place small paillons evenly over the surface. Heat up the metal and, when the solder begins to melt, encourage it to flow over the complete surface by smearing the molten solder with an old saw blade. When it is adequately covered, cool the metal and pickle it. File off any large outstanding lumps of solder. Reflux this metal and the face of the piece to be joined to it. Lay the two pieces of metal face to face and reheat. The solder will remelt and firmly solder one face to another. Look along the edges to make sure the solder has reached them; if not, point the flame at the offending edge, and this will draw the solder out towards it.

COMMON SOLDERING MISTAKES AND POINTS TO REMEMBER

When soldering two halves of a ball together or when making any other kind of cavity, you must always make a very small hole to allow for the expansion and contraction of the air within the cavity. If you do not do this, there are two things that might happen. After a successful soldering the air inside the ball would contract on cooling, and this could cause the solder to be sucked in, leaving a pitted joint. It could also cause thin metal to become distorted. If the soldering was incomplete or if the work had to be reheated at a later stage for any reason, then the air inside would begin to expand as the heating continued – this could cause the work to literally explode, with dangerous results. So remember to leave a hole. This also means that you will have to be especially careful to rinse all the acid from your work after pickling – I usually boil the work in water for 10 minutes to be absolutely sure.

If the solder does not run evenly, it may be due to one or more of several reasons:

(i) the metal or solder is dirty or greasy
(ii) there is inadequate flux
(iii) there is too much flux, which solidifies and forms a barrier
(iv) the metal is not hot enough

The solder may also have been overheated and melted long before the metal to be soldered was hot enough to receive it. This would result in the zinc in the solder burning out or volatizing, thus rendering the solder useless. The solder should not be allowed to melt until the receiving metals are at the correct temperature.

If the two pieces to be soldered are still not joined after the soldering operation has been completed, it may be because the joint was too badly fitting or because the metal did not reach the required temperature. If the solder join breaks apart and has a dry porous appearance, it could be that either the metals were not clean and the solder failed to make a proper contact with the parent metals, or again that the metals were not hot enough to receive the solder. If the solder eats into or pits the metal, then too much heat may have been applied. This happens more commonly with the lower-melting-point solders as these have a higher zinc content, which encourages this pitting.

COMMON SOLDERING SITUATIONS

Although every soldering situation is unique and has its own inherent problems, there are one or two situations which are likely to recur.

When butt-joining (edge to edge) two pieces of metal, it is sometimes difficult to get the solder to run along the joint. In this case, file a small angle along the top inside edge of the pieces (fig. 23). This will form a little channel for the solder to run along.

When joining a circle to a flat, or a circle to a circle, the surface area to be jointed is usually very small and this can result in a weak joint. To avoid this, file a very small flat on the curved faces to be joined (fig. 24). This will considerably increase the surface area to be

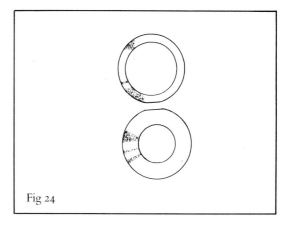

Fig 24 Make a small flat on one side of each of the circles to make a secure joint

joined without visually affecting the curves, thus making a stronger joint.

When soldering a pattern of wires onto a backing plate, it is sometimes difficult to get the wires to touch the metal at every point. To overcome this problem anneal the two together, heating from underneath to prevent the wires overheating. The wires should flatten themselves against the back plate. After pickling, it should be possible to solder them together, again heating from underneath. If, however, the wires are still not touching, 'tack' them together with small bits of solder where they do touch. Allow the metal to cool and then gently tap down the upstanding wires with a hide mallet. Continue to solder as normal.

If small round wires have to be soldered vertically onto a sheet of metal, it can be a little difficult getting them to stay upright. An easy way to overcome this is to drill holes halfway through the thickness of the metal, the holes corresponding exactly in diameter to the size of the wires. The wires can then be pushed into the holes and held firmly while

Fig 23 To solder a butt joint securely, make a small niche along the joint

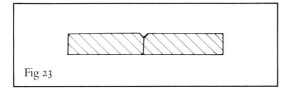

Fig 23

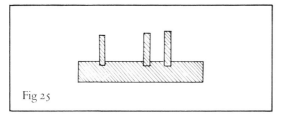

Fig 25

Fig 25 To solder wires more securely on a flat surface, drill holes and push the wires in

they are soldered (fig. 25).

If a rod has to be soldered vertically to a horizontal plate, for example on the back of a cufflink, flux the end of the rod and the spot on the plate to which the rod has to be soldered. Place a paillon of solder on this spot. Holding the rod in a pair of soldering tweezers, heat the cufflink and the rod together without the two actually touching. As the solder begins to flow, press the warmed rod onto the molten solder and remove the source of heat. After a few seconds, the rod can be released from the tweezers and it should be soldered. It is better to have a practice run without the solder, because some people find it difficult to do a different task with each hand. Alternatively you can follow the wiring procedure shown in fig. 21.

If you are joining a circle such as ring shank or bezel, lay the circle down with the joint facing towards you. Proceed to heat the work from the back to the front on each side as this means that the expanding metal is pushed towards the gap, thus closing it even more tightly (fig. 26). If you are soldering links on a chain, push the links not being soldered to one side (fig. 27). This now leaves the joint to be soldered standing well away from the other links, and by pointing the flame away from the other links it should be possible to solder the joints without heating the other links. If necessary, secure the links tightly with pins.

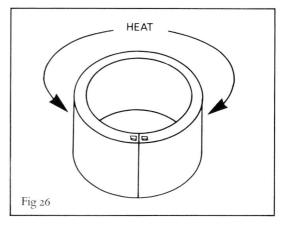

Fig 26

Fig 26 To solder rings, always heat from the back towards the joint

Sometimes, when you are soldering very close to previous solder joints, there is a danger that the first joint may remelt. To prevent this the joint can be painted with an inhibitor, such as powdered rouge or yellow ochre. Obviously great care must be taken not to let the inhibitor touch the new joint to be soldered. As this method is very messy, it is best to use it only in an emergency. If you are very skilful you may never have to use it.

Fig 27 A chain can be arranged like this to solder the links carefully

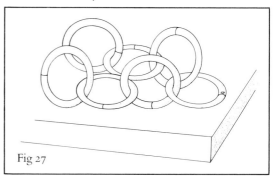

Fig 27

UNSOLDERING

Even after reading this advice, you will undoubtedly at one time or another solder something in the wrong place and will want to remove it. This is always a nerve-racking experience the first time it happens – try to think of it as just another piece of soldering but in reverse. Try to hold the main mass of the metal down by wiring it to a soldering wig or by gripping it in a pair of tweezers. If necessary, rouge the areas not to be unsoldered. Flux the joint needing to be removed and heat as if following a normal soldering procedure. When the solder remelts and shows as a bright line, grip the offending piece in a pair of tweezers and pull it away. You must keep the flame on the joint while you do this – if you remove the flame as soon as you start to pull, the solder quickly re-solidifies. Try not to get the main body of the piece very hot, or you will run the risk of pulling the work in two in the wrong place.

7
Fittings
and Catches

Fittings and catches are both really a case of engineering principles applied in miniature. Consider the problem in hand, i.e. how to pass a cufflink through a small slit yet stop it from falling out once it is there; or how to join or connect one unit to another, making a joint connection move in one, two or more directions. Over the years many traditional principles have been evolved, some of which we use commonly today and some of which have fallen out of favour. By carefully examining jewelry in museums, you may find fittings and catches that you have never seen before but which would be very useful. Some of the most interesting and best-designed ones are those that have been designed to answer a particular problem in a particular piece of work. Whatever answer is arrived at, try to make it visually a part of the design; if the unit cannot be incorporated in such a way that it is hardly visible, then it is better to use it openly and honestly and sometimes it can even be the focal point of the design.

HINGES

A hinge is a unit which enables two pieces of work to be joined in such a way that they can move backwards or forwards but not sideways. It is composed of several lengths of round tubing or chenier, soldered alternately to each side of the work to be joined and then held together by a central pin. There are several kinds of hinges, those that protrude completely like the spine of a book and are in fact commonly referred to as book hinges, those that are partially recessed (called box hinges), and those that are fully recessed and almost invisible (called flush hinges) (fig. 28). Although it is usually very easy to buy the

Fig 28a Book hinge. b Box hinge. c Flush hinge

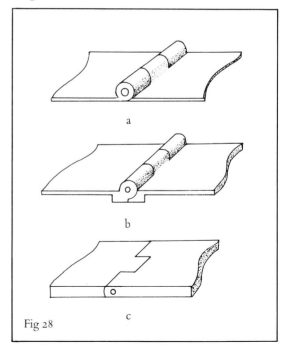

Fig 28

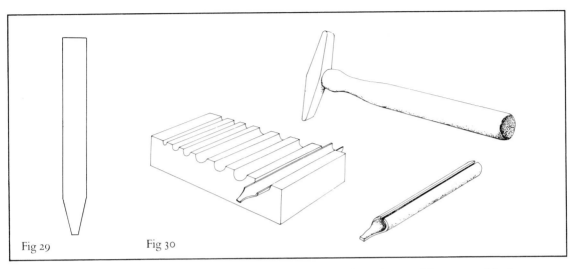

Fig 29

Fig 30

Fig 29 Flat metal cut to shape

Fig 30 Shape the metal in a swage block

chenier, it is useful to know how to make it because very often manufacturers only sell limited lengths and when you need a very short length it can be infuriating.

To make chenier

Roughly calculate the circumference of the finished tube that you require. For the sake of this example, a finished diameter of 3 mm ($\frac{1}{8}$ in) will be required so its circumference will be approximately 9 mm ($\frac{3}{8}$ in) plus a little extra for the thickness of the metal – an extra 1 mm (1/32 in). As it is usual to start the tube large and reduce it to make the bore true, we will start with a strip 15 mm wide and 70 mm long. The metal needs to be fairly thin, in this case 8 BMG – use thicker metal for a larger chenier and thinner for a smaller chenier. Snip the end of the strip into a blunted triangle (fig. 29), and anneal and pickle the metal. The tube now needs to be started off by bending it into a U shape. This can be accomplished by using a swage block (a steel block with U-shaped grooves of

varying sizes), or you can file a groove into a block of hardwood with a round file. Either hammer the length of the metal into a groove with a collet hammer, or use a length of steel rod of suitable diameter and hammer this along the length with a hide hammer. Take the U-shaped strip out and tap the two long edges inwards until the gap is closed as much as possible. Do not attempt to make the tube round at this stage. Make sure the point has become rounded too (fig. 30).

Take a draw plate with holes large enough to take your rough tube, push the triangular point through the relevant hole and pull it through the other side with a pair of draw tongs.

Waxing or oiling the tube makes the operation easier and smoother. Re-anneal and pickle the tube, and repeat the operation until an even bore is obtained. If the diameter of the bore is not critical, then you can continue annealing and drawing down the tube until the correct size is obtained. However, by this method you are likely to make a tube that

71

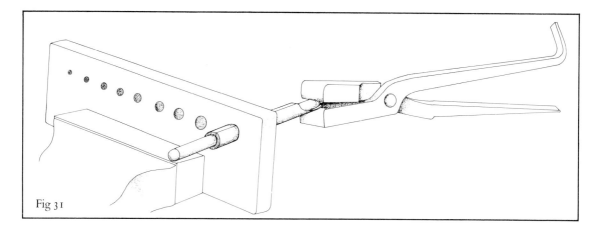

Fig 31

Fig 31 Grasp the chenier and centre rod and pull through a drawplate

has a small bore and thick walls. To control the size of the bore and keep the walls thin, it will be necessary to carry the operation one stage further. Take a length of steel rod or a piano wire that has a diameter corresponding to the internal diameter of the chenier required. Grease or wax it well and push it down into the tube, leaving a few inches protruding. Hammer or punch the blunt point so that it grips the rod securely and proceed to pull the two down together through the draw plate until the tube is gripping the inner rod along its length (fig. 31). If the thickness of the wall is too great, then continue drawing down until it is sufficiently reduced. Because the inner rod is very hard, it will not be affected by the drawing – only the softer silver or gold will be thinned and lengthened.

When the chenier has reached the required size, saw off the blunted point. Take the protruding piece of steel rod and push it into a hole on the draw plate that is large enough for the steel rod to pass through but too small

for the tube, grip the rod in the draw tongs and pull hard – the rod should slide out but it does usually require a fair amount of effort. Re-annealing the tube at this stage will burn out any remaining wax and will also reveal the seam line. You can either solder the seam at this stage, or you can leave it until you are actually soldering the chenier in the hinge unit. If you are making the tube for anything other than hinge chenier, then you should really solder the tube at an earlier stage so that all traces of it will be removed during the drawing-down process.

In jewelry-making hinges are most commonly used for bracelets, (although there are, of course, countless other ways in which they can be used), so for the purpose of this example we will show how to make a flush hinge for a bracelet. This type of hinge must be made from very thick walled tubing, as part of the tube which projects after the hinge is complete will be filed away.

A hinge is normally composed of three or more odd numbers of knuckles – if possible use at least five which makes a more secure joint. Measure the total distance of the hinge required and divide by the number of knuckles. Saw off the lengths, leaving them

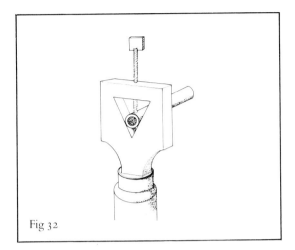

Fig 32

Fig 32 A chenier vice can be used to cut lengths of chenier accurately

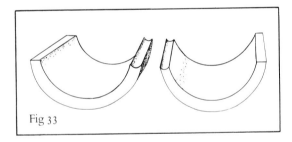

Fig 33

Fig 33 File hollows in each half of the bracelet to receive the chenier

slightly larger to allow for filing. For a hinge to work smoothly and look tidy, each knuckle should have its faces at a right angle to its length. There is a tool called a chenier vice that will make this task easier (fig. 32). To use it, place each length of tube into the triangular-shaped vice gap with one face slightly protruding beyond the flat face of the vice. Tighten the screw just enough to hold the tube – do not screw too tightly or the tube may become distorted. Using a smooth flat file, file the end of the tube until it is level

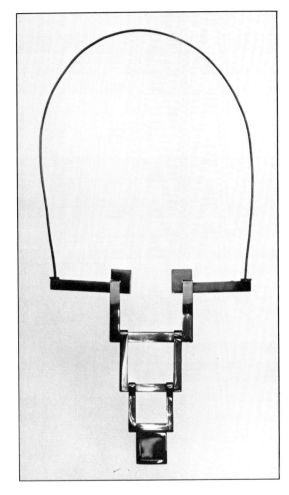

Silver necklace designed in such a way that the square slot-in catch at the front has been made a decorative feature. Designed by Jean England

with the vice face – this end will now be flat and at a right angle to its length.

File away any burr that may be thrown up as a result of the filing. Prepare each half of the bracelet to receive the knuckles by filing a rounded groove as in fig. 33. You can use a round file or a gapping file, which is a flat piece of metal with half-rounded files along each edge – this is better than a round file because the file area is perfectly parallel and does not taper. A round file can only be used for short lengths, and for longer lengths you will have to use a gapping file. The grooves should have a depth of about one-third of the diameter of the chenier, so that when both sides of the bracelet are closed around the chenier about one-third remains exposed.

Now comes the difficult part of soldering on each of the knuckles in the right place and on the right half. The easiest way to do it is to push a steel rod through all the knuckles and place them between the grooves, or bearers, on the bracelet, which should be in the closed position (see fig. 34). Pass binding wire around the whole bracelet to secure it tightly. On the first knuckle paint a minute amount of flux along the joint on the left – do not paint right up to the ends. On the second knuckle paint the flux on the right, on the third knuckle paint it on the left, and so on until every knuckle has been painted. Then place a small paillon on each fluxed knuckle joint, not enough to flow completely along the joint but just enough to tack it into place. If necessary, the other unfluxed side of the knuckle can be painted with rouge or

another inhibitor. Slowly heat up the whole bracelet, making sure the solder does not jump away, and continue heating until the solder melts and begins to flow, then *stop heating immediately.* The solder must not be allowed to reach the end of the knuckle as it may run onto the next knuckle, which should of course only be fixed on the opposite side.

Now pull out the steel rod and take apart the bracelet. Support each half so that the knuckles are in a perfectly horizontal position. Place a little more solder onto each tacked-on knuckle and solder them more securely. Soldering a hinge this way ensures that each knuckle fits tightly alongside the next one, without any danger of soldering the whole hinge together.

Alternatively each knuckle length can be marked with a scribe along the bearer edge and soldered on separately – this method has the advantage of ensuring that knuckles cannot be mistakenly soldered to the wrong side, but it also has the disadvantage of being more difficult to do accurately.

All that remains is for the knuckles to be riveted together. This can be done with either a solid rod or another piece of tubing that fits tightly inside the hinge. A piece of tubing is often neater and easier to fit, but the principle is the same for both. The object is to push the rod or tube down inside the hinge (leave 50 mm (2 in) protruding from each end) and flare out the ends to prevent it from falling out. With the tube this is easily achieved by either burnishing the ends over or gently tapping with a tool similar to the one illustrated (fig. 35) – you can make this tool from any piece of nickel or steel. By tapping down on the tool, the metal is pushed down and out over the edge of the hinge. In the case of a solid rod, just hammer the protruding end to spread the metal – hold

Fig 34 Use binding wire to secure the hinge inside the bracelet

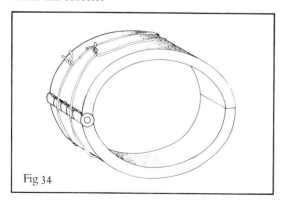

Fig 34

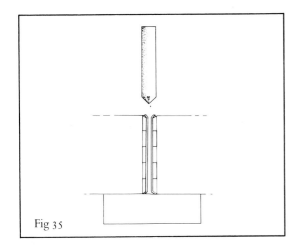

Fig 35 To secure a hinge with tubing, flare out the ends as illustrated

the hinge on a steel block, not on the wooden bench or the rivet will sink into it (fig. 36). To make the ends even neater the hinges can be slightly countersunk so that the finished rivet is flush. The protruding parts of the hinge on the inside and outside should be filed down until the hinge is flush with the bracelet. All that should be seen is a neat castellated line.

These methods of riveting can be used to

Fig 36 To secure a hinge with a solid rod, spread the ends of the rod out

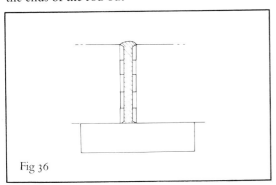

Fig 36

rivet any materials together, (for example silver, ivory, titanium or tortoiseshell. If one of the materials is a metal that can be soldered, for example silver, then one end of the rivet can be soldered to the metal. The materials obviously have to be riveted together in the correct position. An easy way to accomplish this with materials that cannot be soldered together is to drill through the materials simultaneously. If one of the materials is silver or gold and the rivets are to be soldered to it, use the following procedure. Drill the holes in the non-metallic material first, place this over the silver in the correct position and push a pin through the holes to mark the position of the rivet on the silver. When you remove the top material, you will be able to see the places where the rivets need to be soldered.

Sometimes it is not possible to hide the rivets, in which case it is better to use them as an integral part of the design – I have seen pieces of silver and titanium riveted together with little dots of gold that formed a pattern on the two materials. The hinge principle can be adapted to form a catch, and this is simply achieved by using the central riveting rod as a link. The rod is attached by means of a small chain to the main body of the jewelry and can be slipped in and out of the hinge, enabling it to be opened and closed (fig. 37). A ball or some other device needs to be attached to one end of the rod to prevent it from slipping through completely.

Other methods of providing a moving link are based on the simple interlocking of two or more rings (fig. 38). The permutations for this are endless – the rings can be whole or half rings, they can be square or oval, similar or dissimilar in size. The rings may be made very small and unobtrusive, or they can be designed as an important and integral part of the whole piece.

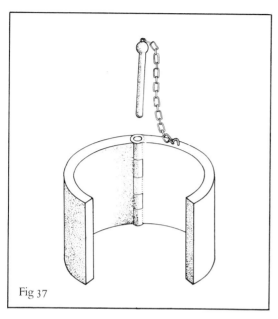

Fig 37

Fig 37 A hinge may also be used as a catch if the centre pin is removable

Fig 38 A few variations on the basic link

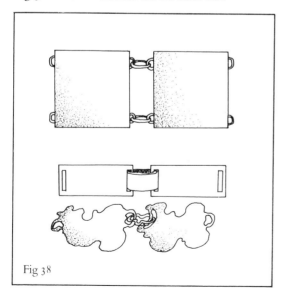

Fig 38

PENDANT FITTINGS

Pendants need something by which they can be attached to the necklace. Obviously this will depend to some extent on the form the necklace takes – a stiff wire collar will have different requirements to a flexible chain, and these will have to be considered when designing the pendant. The fittings may consist of simple-shaped rings soldered onto the top or back of the pendant, or they may be integrated into the design of the pendant. Fig. 39 shows just a few simple examples. If you are a beginner, try to avoid the all-too-easy way out of simply drilling a hole in the top of the pendant – this is rarely a satisfactory answer as the hole will look glaringly out of place. Some pendants can also be worn as brooches, in which case the appropriate fittings should be soldered on.

BROOCH FITTINGS

There are many manufactured brooch fittings available on the market which are usually very satisfactory. However, you may wish to make your own and they are really very easy (as you will see). Whichever kind you decide to use, brooch fittings are composed basically of three components: a hook or catch to receive the pointed end of the pin, the pin itself and the hinge, to which the other end of the pin is attached. The fittings should be soldered onto the brooch slightly above the halfway mark – this is to ensure that the brooch lies close to the body. If it were top heavy it would swing backwards and forwards every time the wearer moved. With the back of the brooch facing you, the hinge should be on the right and the hook or catch on the left. The open side of the hook should face downwards so that the pin cannot be pulled out by the weight of the brooch. Many hinges have a little tab attached to one

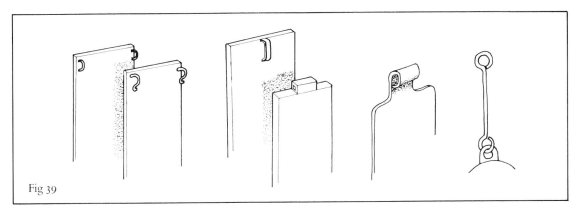

Fig 39

Fig 39 Some examples of simple pendant fittings

side of them, and this should be fixed so that the tab is vertical and facing towards the hook – it acts as a pivot point which will help to make the pin springy. To fit the pin, see below.

To make brooch fittings

Although there are variations, for instance safety catches or two pins, the basic brooch fittings consist of a hook, pin and hinge and you will see many types which you can easily copy.

The simplest hook is a C shape with the top curled under (fig. 40). This can be made of wire or sheet. Although the size of the fittings are related to the size of the brooch, try to keep them small, 3–4 mm ($\frac{1}{8}$ in) high, or they will make the brooch stand away from the body. With this particular hook, the pin will slide upwards along the inside back of the C and will rest on the little curl, so make sure the diameter of the curl is large enough to hold the pin. Using 1–2 mm ($\frac{1}{16}$ in) diameter chenier make a hinge of three units, totalling not more than about 5 mm ($\frac{3}{16}$ in) in length. Using thin sheet – 12 gauge or 1 mm ($\frac{1}{16}$ in) – make an L shape that is as

long as the total length of the hinge. The two sides of the L shape should be slightly higher than the diameter of the hinge chenier – 3 mm ($\frac{1}{8}$ in). Using hard solder, join the two outside hinge units into the L, as shown (fig. 40). This can now be soldered with easy solder to the right-hand side of the back of the brooch. The hinge unit should be soldered with one of the flat sides as the base and the other side facing the centre – this side will now act as a pivot for the pin (the pin must always be very hard and springy).

If the brooch is made of non-precious metals, the pin can be made from nickel silver. If the brooch is made of silver, you can use either 9 carat hard white gold or silver

Fig 40 The components of a brooch fastening showing the C-shaped hook, the pin and the hinge

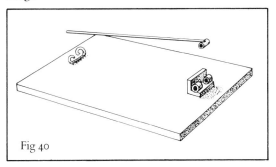

Fig 40

wire. If you are using silver wire, then grip the pin between two pairs of pliers and twist it several times – this will harden the wire and make it springy. If the brooch is made of gold, use the corresponding carat of hard white gold. Hard white gold is, as its name suggests, a very hard alloy enabling you to make thin but very strong pins. The pins should be 0·75 mm–1 mm ($\frac{1}{32}$ in) in diameter. Cut off a length of the wire that extends from the other edge of the hinge to the outer edge of the hook – do not let it protrude beyond the edge of the brooch.

The end of the pin should be shaped so that it will slide easily through the material without leaving ugly holes or cutting the thread. The best shape is a bullet head, rather than a long tapering point (fig. 41). A bullet shape will make a hole by parting the threads of the material, which will close up after the pin has been withdrawn; in contrast, the tapering point is not only dangerous but will cut the fibre threads, leaving the hole behind. The point can be easily and safely polished by rotating it first between a folded piece of polishing paper and then between a folded piece of leather covered with rouge. The

Fig 41 Wrong and right pin-head shapes

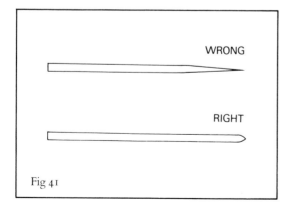

Fig 41

third and middle section of the hinge should be soldered to the blunt end of the pin. To make a stronger joint, file a round groove across the end of the pin so that the chenier will rest securely in the groove while it is being soldered.

All that now remains is to rivet the three hinge units together. Select a piece of wire slightly larger in diameter than the internal diameter of the hinge chenier and file a slight taper on it. Push the wire through the hinge until it jams tightly. Cut off the surplus wire, leaving about 0·5 mm ($\frac{1}{64}$ in) protruding on each side. You can now spread the ends of the rivet, either by tapping them with a tiny watchmaker's hammer or by simply squeezing the rivet. To do this grip the hinge in a pair of parallel pliers – because the ends of the rivet wire protrude, the pliers will in fact only be gripping the wire. Now squeeze the pliers gently and roll them backwards and forwards to spread the ends of the rivet. Do not squeeze the hinge itself. The pin should be able to move freely up and down, and a small amount of pressure should be needed to press the pin downwards on the pivot so that the point of the pin can slide under the hook – when the pressure is released, the pin should spring upwards inside the hook.

Heavy brooches should be secured with a double pin similar to the one in fig. 42. The hook is composed of two C shapes facing each other closer together than the two pins, which are squeezed together and then released inside the two hooks so that each pin is pushing outwards against a hook. The pins are made of one length of wire bent into a U shape. This time, instead of using a hinge, the pins are held in place by the vertical side of an L-shaped angle bent over to hold the pins. This should be done after the angle has been soldered to the brooch, or the heat will anneal and soften the pin.

BRACELET AND NECKLACE FASTENINGS

Again there are many manufactured fittings available, ranging from simple bolt rings to box snaps. If you use a fastening that is in some way spring loaded, be careful when attaching it not to heat the spring which will lose its temper and cease to 'spring'. The permutations on the hook-and-eye principle are endless and can be varied in shape to suit the design. Fig. 43 shows a few of the most common examples.

The double hook principle is the one most often used for the solid necklets popular today. The ball ends can be soldered on or, easier still, can be melted directly onto the wire. To do this, hold the straight length of wire vertically. Dip the end in borax and apply a small flame to the end of the wire until it melts, when it will begin to curl up into a ball. Be careful not to slant the wire, or the ball will form to one side of the wire. If necessary, the ball can be trued up afterwards. The hooks should be formed with round pliers, remembering that one hook should be formed at a right angle to the other. Another simple fastening is that based on a bar and ring. The bar and ring can be any shape as

Fig 42 A double brooch pin for heavy brooches

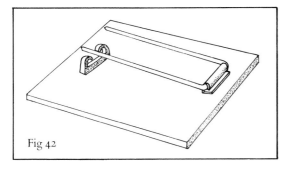

Fig 42

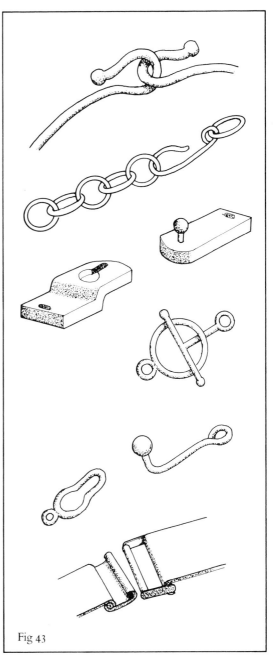

Fig 43

Fig 43 A selection of bracelet and necklace fastenings

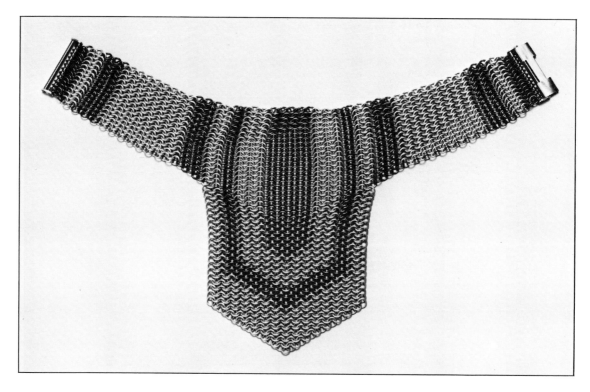

Chainmail necklace – note the bold catch.
Designed by Lexi Dick

long as the bar can be passed through the ring.

Then there are the keyhole fastenings, where a ball is pushed up through a hole, which narrows down into a slot – the ball is then pulled along the slot and cannot escape.

The more complicated fastenings usually incorporate springs or tensioned metal. They can be made very unobtrusive by being fitted on the underside of the necklace or bracelet components so that they are almost invisible. The square box snap and round barrel catch shown (fig. 44) are the basis of many more complicated catches that you can devise for yourself.

The box snap should be cut out of thin

metal and assembled following fig. 45. It is essential that all the angles should be true and square. Instead of just folding the bottom box part, which would give rather rounded corners, you can make sharp angles by filing a right angle along the fold lines with a square needle file. The angle will need to go at least three-quarters of the way through the thickness of the metal. The width of the snap should correspond exactly to the width of the entrance of the box. The snap should be very hard. Again you should use hard white gold with precious metals and nickel with non-precious metals. If you have to use silver, then it must be burnished afterwards to make it hard.

A burnisher is usually an elliptical tool with a very highly polished surface, which is lubricated with spit and rubbed backwards

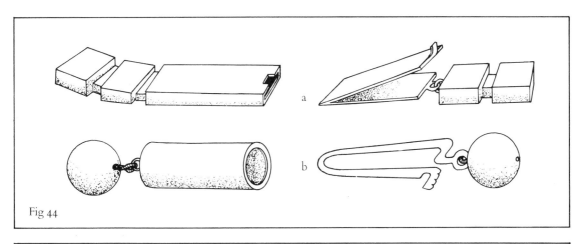

Fig 44

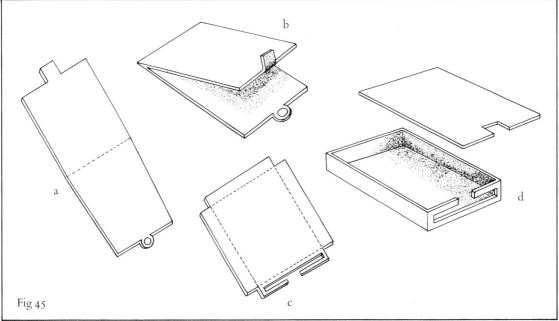

Fig 45

Fig 44a Box snap and b barrel catch

Fig 45a Cut out the flat shape of the box snap.
b Fold up the tab and fold in half. c Cut out the
box shape. d Fold up and solder on a top

and forwards firmly along the metal. This has
the effect of both polishing and hardening the
metal. It will help if you push a piece of
folded paper between the snap while you
burnish it. If the snap does not 'snap' into the
box, increase the angle until it does.

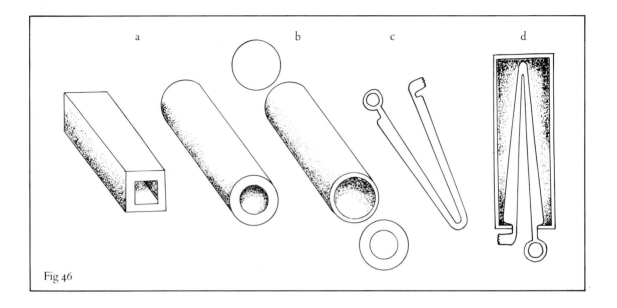

Fig 46

Fig 46a Barrel snaps may be round or square.
b Solder a disc on one end and a circle on the
other. c Flat cut-out shape of snap. d Cross-
section of the snap inside the catch

Although the box and snap can be attached
to the necklace or bracelet with a simple hole
and ring, it will look far neater with a hinge.
The box part can be fixed solidly on the
underside of the necklace but the snap must
be movable.

Barrel snap

See fig. 46. The barrel snap should be made
from round or square tubing. One end is
completely blocked with a plate and the
other end has a plate with a square or round
hole in it. The snap must again be made from
a hard metal. The little nicks on each side of
the base of the snap should be slightly wider
than the thickness of the front plate. If the
snap fails to snap into the barrel, widen the
angle.

CUFFLINKS

Cufflink attachments may be articulated or rigid.
Traditional fittings were always articulated
but today rigid fittings are very popular and
usually more in keeping with modern
designs. The back part of the link should be
designed so that it is related to the design on
the front of the link. It is very disappointing
to turn over an interesting cufflink to find a
dull standard shape on the back. With a little
ingenuity it is usually very easy to relate the
back of the link to the front, in fact very
often the back can be a scaled-down version
of the front. The back must be able to pass
sideways through the button hole, but not
fall out when in position. If a rigid fitting is
to be used, the front and back can be joined
with a rod of whatever section you would
like, as long as it can withstand the pressure
of being leaned on. The rod may be straight
or slightly curved, which sometimes helps the
link to settle across the cuffs. Fig. 47 shows
some of the more common methods of links.

There is a little trick which may help you to solder any long rod shape such as a link to a horizontal base. In the case of the cufflink, the back is soldered to the link with hard or medium solder. Place the back face down on your charcoal block. Put a spot of flux on the centre of the plate and on the end of the rod. Place the paillon of solder on the back plate. Heat this until the solder begins to melt then, without taking the flame away, push the rod onto the spot of molten solder and continue to heat for a few seconds. Take away the flame and allow the joint to cool while still holding the rod in position. This is where a pair of sprung soldering tweezers come in useful, as these will hold the rod without any effort on your part. The other end of the rod can be soldered onto the front by the same method, but this time using easy solder.

Links can also be joined by short lengths of chain or by a combination of rod and chain. The link can be articulated at one or both ends. One of the links in fig. 47 is articulated at the rear end only. The back plate only needs to move sideways, so do not make the hole too large or the back plate will swivel around. Solder the rigid end first. Pass the U-shaped hoop through the hole and lie the rest of the link down flat, so that it does not interfere with the hoop while it is being soldered to the back plate. If the ends of the hoop are perfectly flat and stand up easily, you should have no difficulty in soldering the hoop in position.

EARRINGS

Earfittings can be either for pierced or non-pierced ears. Those for pierced ears can range from simple shaped wires to a rod and butterfly, which is very secure. The earring is soldered to the front of the rod, and the rod is then pushed through the ear and is secured by means of a butterfly (fig. 48a). To make this ear fitting, select a piece of round wire suitable to go through the ear – about 1 mm ($\frac{1}{16}$ in) in diameter and 12 mm ($\frac{1}{2}$ in) long. The wire should be soldered to the earring (fig. 48b). To make the joint more secure,

Fig 47 A selection of cufflink fittings

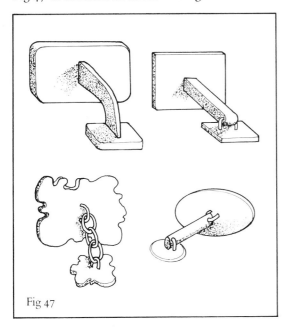

Fig 47

Fig 48a A butterfly earring fastening. b Solder a rod onto the earring.

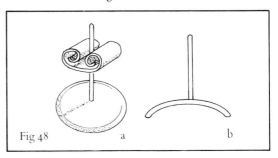

Fig 48   a   b

Rose enamelled brooch designed by Karen
Wagstaff. Photo-etched silver, champlevé
enamelled

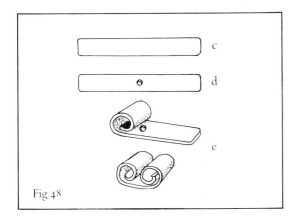

Fig 48

Fig 48c Cut out the flat shape of the butterfly.   d Drill a hole the same size as the rod.   e Roll up each side of the butterfly

drill a hole halfway through the thickness of the earring, the diameter of the hole corresponding to the diameter of the wire (fig. 48d). The wire can now be pushed into the hole and soldered securely.

Cut a strip 3 mm ($\frac{1}{8}$ in) wide and 19 mm ($\frac{3}{4}$ in) long from a thin strip of 3 BMG gauge (0·25 mm) metal. Centre-punch and drill a hole in the centre of the strip. The hole should just allow the wire to be pushed through. With a pair of small roundnose pliers, curl each end inwards (fig. 48e). The two curls should be just under 1 mm ($\frac{1}{16}$ in) apart. Using the same drill as before, push the drill through the hole and between the two curls of the butterfly – this should make a groove in each side. Pinch the two curls together – these should now act as a spring and grip the earring when it is pushed through. A variation of this is to make a screw thread on the end of the wire to which a little stud can be screwed on (fig. 49).

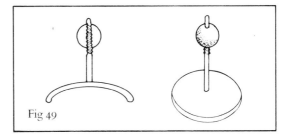

Fig 49

Fig 49 A screw earfitting for pierced ears

To make a screw

Screws and nuts are made with taps and dies. A tap is used to make the internal female thread of the nut, and the die is used to make the external or male thread. Taps and dies are usually bought as a set, which usually also comes complete with a drill of the relevant size. There are different kinds of screws, according to the angle of the thread and the number of threads to the inch. As a jeweller you will only be concerned with the number of threads, and as most of the screws you use will be tiny you need screws with a large number of threads per inch (fig. 50). The high part of the thread is known as the crest

Fig 50 Details of a screw

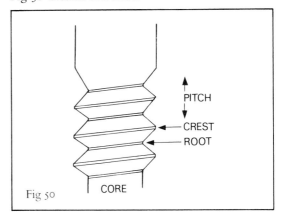

Fig 50

and the low part or groove is known as the root. The pitch is the distance between two adjacent crests. The core is the diameter of the thread from root to root.

From the place where you buy your taps and dies, you should be able to buy a small booklet giving you the number of the set for the diameter of rod or wire that you have. In the case of earrings, the screw should be made from wire that has a diameter of 1·5 mm ($\frac{1}{16}$ in).

To make the screw, take a longer length of the wire than you need and file one end to a right angle. Grip the other end in the vice so that the wire is vertical. The die has a tapered entrance and this should be placed large side down in the die-stock, which is a kind of metal yoke that holds the die. The size of the stock is standard and will hold all the dies, as is the size of the wrench that holds the taps. Rest the die on the top of the wire and gently but firmly begin to turn it in a clockwise direction. It is essential that the stock is always kept at a right angle to the wire being threaded. For this reason it is best to work at eye level. It will help if you lubricate the work with a thin oil.

The nut is made in reverse. It can be made from a piece of round or square rod or any other shaped nut that you would like. Again, hold it securely and vertically in a vice and drill a hole through it to the correct size. Taps usually come in sets of three – taper, intermediate and bottoming tap – thus ensuring that the thread is made gradually, though for the tiny jewellers' screws you really only need the taper and bottoming tap. Lubricate the tap with oil before you use it. Secure the taper tap in the wrench and, holding it perfectly vertical, begin to wind it in a clockwise direction. Because the taper tap is almost smooth to begin with, the progress is initially easy but do not be

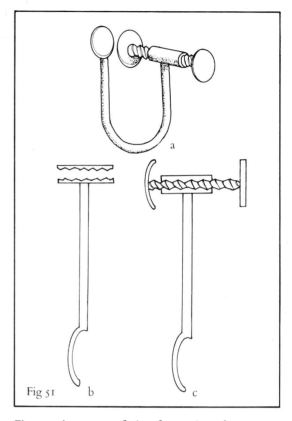

Fig 51

Fig 51a A screw earfitting for unpierced ears. b Assemble the fitting flat. c Wind the screw into the tube and solder the circles onto the ends

tempted to rush or you may break the delicate threads. After a few turns withdraw the tap, clean off the turnings and start again. Repeat this process until the required length has been threaded. Repeat with the other two taps until the thread is complete.

You also need to know how to make a screw if you are to make earfittings for non-pierced ears which screw to fit (fig. 51a). It is easier to make the fitting in a flat length and then bend it up afterwards (fig. 51c). Take a piece of round wire 1·5 mm ($\frac{1}{16}$ in) in diameter and about 25 mm (1 in) long. Either flatten and widen one end by hammering it, or solder on a small round disc 4 mm ($\frac{3}{16}$ in) in diameter. This provides both an anchor point for the earring to be attached to, and makes a cushion for the ear when the fitting is screwed tight. To the other end solder a piece of tube 2·5 mm ($\frac{3}{32}$ in) in diameter and 3 mm ($\frac{1}{8}$ in) long which has been threaded internally (fig. 51b). Make an 8 mm ($\frac{5}{16}$ in) length screw of the corresponding size and screw it into the tube. Onto one end of the screw solder a domed disc 4 mm ($\frac{3}{16}$ in) in diameter and after screwing on the threaded tube, solder a flat disc 4 mm ($\frac{3}{16}$ in) in diameter onto the other end. The domed disc will be placed against the ear and the flat disc will be used as a finger hold. With a pair of half-round pliers, bend the wire into a U shape.

Sprung ear clips

These earfittings are used for non-pierced ears and they are only suitable for stud-type earrings. The unit is composed of two parts, the hinge and the spring. Follow fig. 52 for the method of making. To assemble the earfitting, solder the hinge onto the back of the stud with easy solder. Prise open the two rings, so that the two outside struts of the spring can be squeezed together and released inside the two rings. The longer centre strut should protrude above the upright on the back of the hinge. Squeeze the two rings together securely.

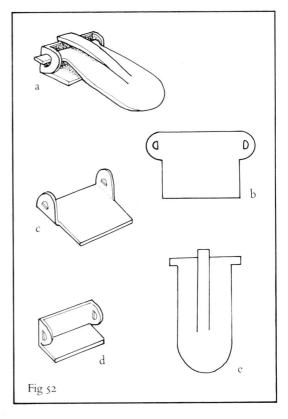

Fig 52

Fig 52a A sprung earclip. b Cut out the flat hinge. c Fold up the tabs. d Fold in half. e Cut out the clip and assemble

Brooch and ring in 18 carat gold, with cloisonné enamel in purple, yellow and red. Based on a Chinese flower painting. Designed by Patti Clarke

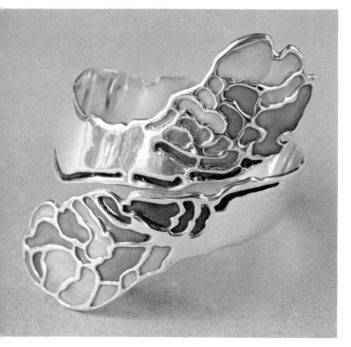

Silver hinged bracelet, champlevé enamelled in transparent enamels. Designed by Patti Clarke

8
Decorative Techniques

One of the most important aspects of jewelry can be its surface decoration – or lack of it. Indeed the decoration can be the jewelry itself. Decoration is one of the easiest ways in which you can define your style, the 'something' that makes your work different from anyone else's. You may find the whole idea of decoration abhorrent – you may like clean, uncluttered lines and this too will be the definition of your style. We will presume, however, that you have decided upon the need for a decorative surface and you now have to decide which technique to use. You can interpret the same design in various ways by the use of different techniques. Some techniques will obviously be more suitable for a particular design, for example, a fine geometric pattern may lose a little of its crispness if you decide to etch it but it could gain more accuracy by engraving. Once you have decided upon the technique, then you must be careful not to destroy the form completely by covering it with decoration. You must try to achieve a balance between the decorated and the undecorated areas so that you give the eye somewhere to rest.

ETCHING

This is a process whereby selected parts of the metal are etched away by acid to form a pattern. The depth and design are variable.

Etching produces a slightly rough, bitten appearance, which can be controlled to some extent by the strength of the acid and the length of time the metal is left in the acid bath. Most metals can be etched, although in the case of gold it is rather an expensive technique because unless you have a costly refining plant the metal eaten away by the acid is lost. In large manufacturing concerns the acid solutions are collected and the metal recycled.

Basically, the technique is to coat the metal with a substance resistant to acid and then to scratch through the resist thereby exposing the bare metal underneath. The work is then immersed in an acid solution and the bare metal will be attacked by the acid and eaten away. After a selected length of time the work is removed from the acid and the resist is cleaned off. The areas which had previously been exposed will now be seen as recesses.

The metal to be etched must be prepared correctly. If at all possible, make the piece of metal to be etched slightly larger than the required finished size – this is in case of mishaps, for often the edges of the metal are accidently attacked by the acid. If the shape has been made slightly larger, this leaves a small allowance that can be filed away to leave a perfect edge.

As the prime motivation for using etching as a decorative technique is its rough, bitten characteristics, obviously any polishing and smoothing down of the surface should be done before the etching or these characteristics may well be altered or removed. The metal surface should therefore be cleaned of scratches and polished in the usual way. If a satin finish is required, then this too must be done now. The edges should be filed smooth, but not polished as they may have to be refiled after etching.

After polishing, wash the metal in ammonia and water to remove any trace of the polishing compound. Any trace of grease will prevent the resist from adhering, so it is important to make sure that the metal is grease free – as an added precaution you can swab it with trichlorethylene or a similar degreasing agent. A satin surface can be rubbed down with steel wool or whiting. Be careful not to handle the metal more than is strictly necessary – hold it in a piece of lint-free cloth. It is now ready for the resist to be applied.

There are many types of resist, varying from simple wax and shellac to commercial mixtures. Most of the commercial mixtures have a pitch base and come in solid or liquid form. I have even seen nail polish used in an emergency! As a general rule, the commercial resists are superior to wax in that finer and more intricate lines can be scratched through the resist. If you are going to use wax, melt it in a large basin – do not let it boil as it may spit quite dangerously. Hold the metal in a pair of tweezers and dip it in the molten wax. Allow the wax to harden and cool, which will take only a few minutes. The bare areas where the tweezers touched can be covered with a brush and molten wax.

With the liquid resist it is a simple matter of painting the liquid onto one side, letting it dry, and painting the other side. It usually takes about 20 minutes for each side to dry. The edges should be painted at least twice

because they are very vulnerable and the resist may easily chip off. Leave the resist to harden so that it may be held without leaving fingermarks. Do not attempt to speed up the drying process by putting the metal near heat – all this does is melt the resist and prolong the process. As the resist tends to deteriorate if the lid is off the bottle, it is better to buy small quantities or decant it into a smaller bottle.

If the resist comes in a solid cake, the metal should be slightly warmed and the cake smeared across the surface. The resist can be spread evenly by means of a dabber, a leather pad which is rocked backwards and forwards across the molten resist to spread it evenly. The metal is then left to cool. This method can obviously only be used on one side of the metal; the other side must be painted with liquid resist or molten wax. As the cake does not appear to have any particular advantages, I always use a liquid on both sides as this seems easier to apply. However, you might prefer the cake.

There is also available a soft resist in cake form which never hardens. This is applied to the surface of the metal in the same way as the hard resist. Different materials can now be pressed into the soft resist, and when pulled away they leave a pattern of the characteristics of the material. Very interesting results can be obtained using this method – try using sacking, lace, string, rope, coarse cork, bark or anything that has an interesting texture.

In the case of the hard resists, all that remains is to scratch the pattern through the resist until the bare metal is exposed. Any tool may be used to scratch the pattern: needles for fine lines, scribes for thicker line or areas. Remember that the pattern being scratched will appear as a recessed area and the remaining area will be in relief. Any areas of metal accidently exposed must be retouched with resist and allowed to dry. Try to carry out the whole etching process within one day, as the resist keeps on hardening and gradually becomes so brittle that it is difficult to scratch a fine line through without other areas flaking off.

The metal can now be lowered into a glass or plastic bowl containing the relevant acid mix (see page 92 for the details of the recipes). Try to use a plastic spatula or other similar instrument, rather than a pair of brass tweezers which may scratch the surface. As the acid begins to bite into the metal, bubbles will rise – if they rise rapidly this means the bite (the action of the acid) is very strong and quick. This will give a very ragged finish and, unless you require this, carefully add a little more water (the acid will already be diluted, so there is no risk of an explosion) until the bubbles rise at the rate you require – experience will teach you the relationship between the rise of the bubbles and the strength of the bite. Obviously, if no bubbles arise then more acid will have to be added. If you see bubbles rising from an area which is supposed to be covered in resist, you will know that you have sprung a leak – take the metal out immediately, rinse and dry it well, then look closely for the offending spot and repaint it with resist. While the metal is in the acid the areas being etched must be brushed with a feather to clear the metal of bubbles and sludge, which cling to the metal and prevent the acid from biting properly – do not forget to rinse the feather in clean water, or you will find that the next time you come to use it it will have rotted away.

The length of time that the acid takes may be anything from a few minutes to an hour, depending on how strong the acid is, how large the exposed areas are and what depth is required. Continual experimenting will help you. Keep checking that all is well by removing the metal from the acid, rinsing it and drying well and then examining it. Test the depth of fine lines with a pin. With etching there is a tendency for the acid to undercut the lines and if the metal is left in for any length of time the lines may widen, and lines placed close to each other may merge. Bear this in mind when selecting the strength of the acid. It may be better to use a weak acid for a long time, rather than a stronger acid which has a tendency to undercut.

When the depth of the bite is enough, remove the resist. Wax can simply be melted off, and most of the asphaltum resists can be removed with turpentine or white spirit. Some other proprietary brands require acetone. If you are unsure, check with the supplier.

There are other ways of using etching, besides the traditional basic way already outlined. Instead of completely covering the surface with resist and scratching away a pattern, thereby etching the negative design, the resist may be applied as the main pattern and the areas left may be etched away, leaving the design in positive. Interesting effects can be achieved by dripping or trailing the resist onto the surface of the metal. The metal may be etched like a bas-relief, in two or more layers, in which case you have to work backwards. The entire design area is exposed to the acid and allowed to etch for a few minutes. When the shallow etch is ready, the area needing only a little etching is painted over with resist and the remaining area is returned to the acid and allowed to etch deeper. Using this method, very intricate and complicated reliefs can be achieved.

By experimenting with the materials and techniques of etching it is possible to discover your own individual approaches.

Recipes

With all recipes containing acid it is essential that you *always add acid to water* and *never* the other way round.

Basic recipe for copper, gilding metal and silver
7 parts water
3 parts nitric acid

Basic recipe for gold
4 parts nitric acid
8 parts hydrochloric acid
1 part perchloride of iron
40 parts water

STAMPING

Stamping or punching can be used to transfer small patterns onto metal. It can even be used to punch a pattern and cut out a shape in one operation. The pattern is engraved quite deeply into the end of a steel or nickel punch, then the punch is placed against the surface of the metal and struck with a hammer.

If a sharp, flat pattern is required the metal is laid on a steel block and stamped, but by placing the metal on a wooden block a softer, slightly dented pattern can be achieved. This can give interesting effects if each design is repeated quite close to the next one with a small space between – the plain space is usually pushed upwards by the downwards stroke of the stamp next to it and the resulting soft bulge catches and reflects the light. The stamp may be used to produce single complete designs or repeated in a formal or informal pattern. The designs may even be overlapped to produce the bark effect which is very popular today.

The metal being stamped may or may not be annealed, according to the effect required. Annealed metal must be used for deeper patterns or the metal may split, but if a shallow, sharp pattern is required then annealed metal may distort too much. It is best to stamp a couple of trial pieces to see the effect produced.

The stamping technique may also be used to produce larger linear designs. Lengths of steel or nickel wire should be twisted into shapes or patterns. The wire shape is then placed onto a sheet of annealed silver or some other soft metal, which should be lying on a steel block. The wire shape is then hammered onto the soft metal, while being held firmly in place. When the wire pattern is removed, it leaves a shallow depression corresponding to the shape of the pattern – again the pattern may be stamped singly, repeated or overlapped.

REPOUSSÉ AND CHASING

Repoussé and chasing are usually bracketed together because they are complimentary and, although sometimes used separately, they are usually used together. They are both methods of moulding soft malleable metals, such as silver, into either shallow or deep relief. Tracing, which is part of the chasing technique, can be used to produce decoration which is entirely linear. Basically, the difference between the two techniques is that repoussé is modelled from the wrong side of the metal and chasing is modelling from the front or right side.

The tools that are needed are repoussé and chasing punches, a chasing hammer and a bowl of pitch to support the metal. The punches, made of forged steel, can be purchased or you can make them yourself – indeed if you become very enthusiastic and concentrate on this technique, it is unlikely

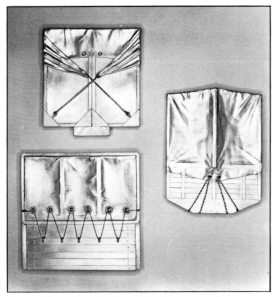

'Lorry' brooches designed by Rosamund Conway. Chased and repousséd in fine silver with 18 carat gold additions

that you will be able to buy every subtle type of punch you require. The punches are quite short – about 10 cm (4 in) – and the ends are shaped according to your requirements. Repoussé tools usually have fuller, rounder profiles which are used to push and stretch the metal out. Chasing tools are generally flatter, as they are used to smooth and planish the shapes pushed out by the repoussé tools. Tracing tools have thin, narrow ends rather like chisels, although they are not used for cutting but as their name suggests for tracing the linear part of the design. Some tracing tools are curved to give a smooth continuous line of curves and sweeps. Matting tools have flat, finely textured ends which are used to texture flat areas of the design and thus provide a contrast to the shiny, rounded areas.

There are other special-purpose tools, used for rings, dots, triangles, etc. The plain-faced tools must be kept highly polished and free

from scratches, as every mark of the punch will be transferred to the silver.

The chasing hammer is designed to be light, as chasing is a lengthy process, and the handle thins considerably at its waist so that the hammer is springy. The large wide head ensures steady and continual contact with the head of the chasing tool.

The metal to be worked must be supported from behind by a material that is resilient enough to support the metal, but soft enough to allow the metal to be stretched and pushed into its surface – pitch is the material that has commonly been used for hundreds of years. Commercially prepared chasing pitch may be obtained, but it is quite easy to mix your own. The basic compound is pitch (Swedish pitch if you can get it), which must then be added to according to the state in which it arrives. You should be able to get pitch from your local road-working department. Plaster of paris or any other commercial filler is added to give more body to the pitch, and if it is very hard, tallow is added to make it softer. During hot weather the mixture will get even softer, so it is better to make it slightly on the hard side.

Basic recipe for pitch
2 parts pitch
1 part plaster of paris

Melt the pitch slowly over a gas ring and stir well. When it is molten add the plaster of paris. Do not overheat the pitch or it will become brittle. Be careful not to get any molten pitch onto yourself – it is extremely hot and sticks to the skin, causing a very painful burn. If you should get any molten pitch on your skin, immediately put the affected part under cold running water, which will cool the pitch and prevent it from burning any further – do not attempt to rip off the pitch sticking to you, for at the moment it will be acting as a sterile bandage. Go straight to a doctor or casualty department who will know how to deal with it.

The molten pitch should then be poured into a receptacle of a suitable size. As far as jewelry is concerned, its small size can be coped with in a standard-size pitch bowl – a hemispherical cast iron bowl about 205 mm (8 in) in diameter. As it is unlikely that you will require the full depth, it is more economical to half fill the bowl with clean pebbles. The pitch bowl is usually supported on a leather or wooden collar, which enables the bowl to be easily tilted in any direction while at the same time you hold the work securely. If you have small, fairly flat pieces to do, then a quantity of pitch can be smeared onto a block of wood which can then be held in a universal vice.

The metal to be modelled should be clean and freshly annealed and pickled. The thickness of the metal depends to some extent on the depth to which the design is to be repousséd. If considerable relief is required, then 6 or 8 BMG (approximately 0.5 mm ($\frac{1}{64}$ in) should be used. You can use even thinner metal (if you ever have a chance, look at the back of one of those heavily embossed Victorian dressing table sets – the metal is barely thicker than a milk bottle top!).

Gently warm the surface of the pitch – do not let it catch fire as this will char the pitch and make it gritty. If the temperature is very low, you can gently warm the metal also. Press the metal onto the molten pitch. Do not melt the pitch too much or the metal will sink beneath the surface – allow the pitch to cool sufficiently for you to press on the metal without it sinking further (fig. 53a). Draw the design onto the metal and then redraw the design with a scribe – not too deep or the

marks will show later. The traditional procedure is to then work over the scribe marks with a tracing tool. If the design is very rounded, use a curved tracing tool.

The punch is held between the thumb and first two fingers – the remaining fingers are used to support the hand and tool at a steady angle to the metal. Hold the tool upright but pointing away from the body so that as you work you can see clearly the line that you are following. Move the tool slowly along the line, tapping quickly with the hammer. Do not strike too hard or you may cut the metal – should this occur, run a little hard solder along the cut the next time you have to anneal the silver. When tapping do not look at the hammer head – it is broad enough to make contact easily – just concentrate on the line that you are following.

The next step is to work from the wrong side of the metal, pushing out the areas to be embossed. To lift the metal from the pitch, warm the surface gently and push a blunt flat rod under one of the edges to lever the metal away from the pitch. The pitch can be removed by either wiping with paraffin or

---

Fig 53a Hold the thin sheet of metal to be repousséd in a pitch bowl.

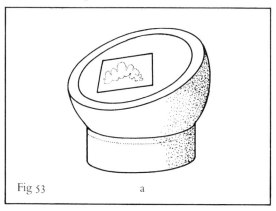

Fig 53   a

burning off – as the metal will need continual re-annealing, this latter method is probably the easiest. Each time the metal is annealed, the pitch gradually burns off and is reduced to an ash which should fall off after quenching. The metal must now be pickled. You must anneal the metal every time it begins to harden, or the silver may easily split.

Replace the silver, traced side down, onto the molten pitch. Take the relevant repoussé tools and begin to stretch and mould the metal. It is usually necessary to strike the tool more firmly in repoussé than in tracing. Do not use a repoussé tool that is much smaller than the finished shape you require, or you may get a slightly dimpled effect. Keep the repoussé tool constantly moving backwards and forwards over the metal so that each stroke is overlapped – this will help to give a smoother curve. If the metal begins to harden, remember to remove it from the pitch and re-anneal it. When you have worked sufficiently from the back, turn the metal over and chase from the front.

It is very important when placing partially embossed metal onto the pitch to make sure that the pitch wells up inside every cavity – if you fail to do this, you may flatten the hollow shapes when you come to chase them from the front. Hollows can be detected by a dull sound. The purpose of the chasing is to refine the shapes produced by the repoussé. The slightly flatter tools should be moved quickly over the surface while they are being tapped. This should smooth out the shapes and flatten any stray dimples. The edge of the tool can be used to define the point where the convexity joins the background. It will usually be necessary to keep working from one technique to the other until the piece is complete. Any texturing to be done with matting tools should be left until the last moment, as mistakes made with these tools are extremely difficult to disguise.

Although the method just outlined is the the accepted traditional way, it is by no means necessary to follow it implicitly. For instance, you may not like the hard edge given by the tracing tool or the rather mechanical finish of the matting tool. By experimenting, you will find the method that suits your design. Once people have tried repoussé they seem to get bitten by the bug and continue to use it. There is something very pleasurable about seeing the work moulded in one continuous process before one's eyes. If you wish to work on hollow objects such as beads, fill them with molten pitch and work as before – it is rather a tedious business as the pitch has to be completely melted out if the metal is to be re-annealed.

ENGRAVING

Of all the decorative techniques, engraving is perhaps the one that needs most skill and practice to produce work of even a tolerable standard. It is really quite difficult to master, and if you really want to learn engraving seriously you should attend a class where this technique is specifically taught. It is, however, a very useful technique to be able to use, not only for the obvious purpose of decoration but for stone setting, enamelling and just the general tidying up of one's work.

Engraving is a method of cutting away a thin sliver of metal to produce either very fine lines or small areas. Because the metal is cut, it has an accurate, definite edge. The cut metal also catches and reflects the light, increasing its sparkling characteristics.

The tools that are used are called gravers – you may sometimes hear them referred to as burins, a rather more old-fashioned name. They are made from very hard, thin rods of steel and come in many different sizes and sections, varying from the most commonly used square section to round, oval, flat, knife edge and many others. All these profiles also come in graduating sizes. The handle is a small, rounded mushroom shape with one flat side, which fits comfortably in the palm of the hand. The handle and graver are bought separately, so the length can be adjusted to suit you personally. It is most important that the length is correct so that good control can be maintained. To hold the tool, press the wooden handle into the palm of your hand and grip the metal rod between your thumb and first two fingers (fig. 53b). The thumb will be used as a guide for the graver to press and slide against. When held correctly, the tool should just protrude beyond the end of your fingers.

If the tool is too long, the best way to

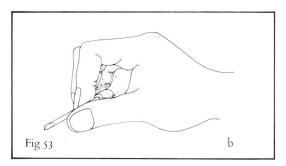

Fig 53   b

Fig 53b Tuck the handle of the graver firmly into your palm and hold the metal between finger and thumb

shorten it is to grind a waist at the point to be broken off (at the handle end). Grind only a little at a time, taking care not to overheat the metal or it will lose its temper. When a waist of about 3 mm ($\frac{1}{8}$ in) is left, snap the piece off – wrap the tool in a rag, clamp it in a vice with the surplus protruding, grip the surplus in a pair of pliers and twist sharply. The rag will prevent stray splinters.

The tool will now have to be ground and honed – even if the graver was the correct length, you will need to sharpen the tip because a dull edge will cut badly and inefficiently. It is generally accepted that the best angle for the tip is 45 degrees, although in practice you may find that you have to alter this slightly for particular requirements.

As you will never need the full depth of the front face, it is wasteful to have to grind this away every time the tool needs sharpening. Instead grind away a section on top, tapering off towards the handle – about 25 mm (1 in) should be enough. Now grind the front face of the graver to an angle of 45 degrees on an oilstone lubricated with a little thin oil. Refine this face by using an Arkansas stone, which gives an extremely fine finish.

Most of the gravers can be left at this point, but if you are going to engrave on curved surfaces you will have to grind away a small facet underneath either side of the point. This

9 carat gold engraved bracelet. Designed and engraved by Malcolm Appleby

is only normally done to the square graver. If the graver picks up a nick on your nail (the traditional way of testing), then it is sharp enough. To keep it sharp, push the end into a cork when it is not in use.

There is a traditional way of transferring the design to be engraved onto a sheet of metal. Rub a wedge of plasticine over the metal, thus depositing a layer of slightly gritty grease. Now rub a pencil over the back of the drawing, making sure that it is evenly covered. Place the paper on the metal with the graphite touching the greasy surface and retrace the drawing. The grease underneath will pick up the graphite from the paper. Remove the paper and lightly retrace the graphite lines with a scribe.

An alternative method is to take a sheet of thin, clear acetate, place it over the design and trace the design onto the acetate with a sharp instrument like a scribe, which makes a deep groove in the acetate. When the tracing is complete, turn the sheet over and you will see that the tracing appears as sharply raised lines, and if you rub a pencil over the tracing the raised lines will catch the graphite. The sheet should now be placed on the plasticine-covered metal and rubbed firmly across its surface with a burnisher or roller, when the graphite will be transferred to the metal.

A professional engraver will have tools such as an engraver's block, which is a complicated instrument for holding the job at any angle that may be required. But for our purposes an ordinary sandbag will suffice. Press the work onto the bag and hold it with your fingers well away from the cutting area. If the metal to be engraved is very small, you can stick it to a block of wood with sealing wax and hold this in a universal vice.

The graver is held in the other hand in the position already described. To start off, press the point of the graver into the metal, at the same time lowering the tool and pressing forwards. You will need something to practise with and a good discipline is a rather ornate alphabet set – this will give you straights and curves. To engrave a curve or a circle, turn the work and not the graver. If you are engraving properly, you will raise a sliver of metal up in front of the graver – if it falls to one side, then you are holding the graver at a slight angle and you must correct it. To finish your stroke and break off this sliver, simply flick the graver upwards. You can produce special effects with different tools, and by swaying the tool from side to side you can produce a wavy effect.

One of the typical beginner's mistakes is to slip and run the line farther than you intended. If the line is shallow, it can be removed by burnishing or by grinding away the mark with a Water of Ayr stone and repolishing. But if the mistake is very deep and large, it will have to be filled with solder and resmoothed – failing that, the whole surface will have to be filed away and you will have to start again.

NIELLO

If you have learnt how to etch or engrave, you will now be able to use niello as a decorative technique. This is a very old technique used by the ancient Persians, Egyptians and Romans. It has always been very popular with gunsmiths for the decoration of guns.

Niello is a dense black metallic mixture which is used to fill depressions in the work and is fused by heat. It derives its attraction from the beautiful contrast of the black niello and the colour of the parent metal, which is usually silver although it can also be applied to gold, copper, bronze and steel.

Unfortunately, it is difficult to obtain

commercially prepared niello in the West and it usually has to be mixed in the workshop, a rather smelly and slightly dangerous process. The fumes given off by the process are toxic, so do not prepare niello in a confined area, although the small quantities you are likely to need should not prove too dangerous.

Old jewelry and silversmithing manuals give a variety of recipes for niello. They all use basically the same ingredients but by varying the amounts slightly different colours can be obtained, such as purplish black or bluish black. However, in practice it seems very difficult to control these variations – you should experiment and see what you can do, but remember that a large lead content makes the niello grey and difficult to grind. This recipe is a good basis from which to start:

Basic recipe for niello
1 part silver
2 parts copper
3 parts lead
12 parts flowers of sulphur

The ingredients together produce silver sulphide, copper sulphate and lead sulphide, which will combine at low temperatures.

To mix the ingredients, put all the metals in a crucible and place it in a kiln until all the metals have melted, stirring them with a long wooden stick (do not worry about the slight charring). When they are properly mixed, stir in the flowers of sulphur and return the crucible to the kiln. Remelt the metals and stir again. When everything has been thoroughly mixed, take the crucible out of the kiln and pour the mixture into a small ingot mould, if you have one. If not, carve a long finger-like depression into a fire brick or charcoal block. The niello is easier to break off in small quantities from a long, thin rod rather than a thick block.

The niello deteriorates when ground, so it is better to grind it only as you need it. If you do not have a kiln, you can melt the mixture with a strong blowtorch or a large propane flame. In this case melt the metals one at a time, first the copper, then the silver and finally the lead. Mix well, add the flowers of sulphur and proceed as before. The niello should be stored in a plastic bag or airtight container.

Preparation of the metal
As niello is the last technique that should be carried out on an article of work, the piece of jewelry should be complete except for polishing. No other heating or soldering can be accomplished after the niello has been applied, as the lead content will eat into the parent metal.

To enable the niello to be applied to the jewelry, a depression of some kind must be made to hold the mixture. This depression can be made by engraving, stamping, chasing, etching or any other suitable method. If the design incorporates large areas, make sure that the depression is of an even depth as any high points may show through the niello. After the design to be filled is complete, the metal should be cleaned and degreased by pickling and washing it in ammonia. A glass fibre brush is very useful to scratch the surface of the depression to expose clean metal underneath. Avoid handling the article of work any more than is necessary.

A small piece of niello must now be ground down into small particles that can be laid into the depressions. To save time, smash the niello with a hammer between two sheets of thick paper and then transfer the pieces to a pestle and mortar. Add a little water and grind the niello to small, even particles. If it has a high lead content, you will find it impossible to grind as the mixture will be too soft. In that case, rub the niello against an old coarse file and then mix the filings with a little water. Any tools that you have used for niello should be reserved for this work as the lead particles will contaminte the tools and may easily be transferred to other work. This also applies to the pestle and mortar.

Paint borax in the depressions and then fill them with the ground, wet niello. The water is only to make the filling easier. The niello can be applied with a feather quill or a metal spatula.

Pack the niello in tightly and slightly overfill the cavity, as the mixture will sink when molten. Suck away surplus water with a corner of blotting paper and leave the mixture somewhere warm to dry – if the mixture is still wet when heated, it will splutter as the water boils out and the niello will be disturbed. If you have a kiln, place the article on a support and put it gently in the kiln, taking care not to spill the niello. As the metal warms, the mixture will melt and fuse to the silver. If the kiln has a peephole watch through this, if not leave the door slightly open. The moment the niello has melted properly, take the article out – do not allow it to overheat as the niello will bubble and eat into the parent metal. If you do not have a kiln and the piece of work is flat, it may be heated from underneath with a torch – make sure it is heated evenly.

Allow the jewelry to cool naturally. If any of the areas are too low, refill them and refire carefully. When all the areas have been filled satisfactorily, the surplus niello should be filed away – file the niello until it is level with the base metal. Smooth with fine emery or Water of Ayr stone. If the areas of niello are shallow, be careful not to overfile or you will break through the shallow layer. The whole piece of work can then be polished as usual. If possible, polish by hand as machine polishing may wear down the softer niello.

ENAMELLING

Enamelling is a very complicated technique and if you wish to do it very well you will be wise to read a book completely devoted to the subject. There is not sufficient space in this book to cover more than the basic technique.

Enamelling has always had a particular attraction for me because of the way in which it enables one to introduce colour into

Brooch using a variety of techniques: repoussé cloud, cloisonné enamelled balloon, and a twisted wire-work basket. Designed by Joan Russell-Williams

jewelry in a permanent way – almost every imaginable shade and hue is obtainable. It is an extremely old technique, and was used by the ancient Romans and Greeks. It has achieved various heights of popularity during the past, notably the Mughal era in India when extremely delicate enamelling was carried out. During the eighteenth century in Limoges in France, an extremely skilled form of painted enamel was named after the town in which it was perfected.

Basically, enamel is a form of soft glass known in the basic state as flux. It is coloured by the addition of metallic oxides and is obtainable in transparent, translucent, opaque and opalescent forms. Today it is possible to buy enamels in a wide range of colours – you can also mix your own, but that is not normally necessary. The enamel is bought in either a lump form, known as frit, or ready ground as a fine grit. If you can, buy the enamel in the lump form because it will keep better – it deteriorates in continuous contact with the atmosphere. The enamels are ground very finely and then applied to the metal according to whichever method you are using, then fired in a kiln until the enamel melts and fuses to the metal.

There are various methods of enamelling but the basic ones are as follows:

Cloisonné
This was the method used in ancient jewelry. The enamel is held in place and one colour is separated from another by small round or flat wires. The wires are tacked on with small pieces of solder to hold them in place, or a layer of flux can be laid first on the base metal and fired – the wires should then be laid in place on top of the flux and refired. The flux remelts and adheres to the wires. The recesses are then filled with the desired colours and refired (fig. 54a).

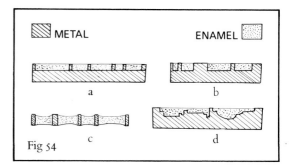

Fig 54a Cross-section of cloisonné enamel. b Cross-section of champlevé enamel. c Cross-section of plique-à-jour enamel. d Cross-section of basse-taille enamel

Champlevé
With this method the recesses to hold the enamel are carved in some way out of the parent metal. They can be made by etching, engraving or stamping; they can also be made by piercing out one sheet of metal and soldering it to another base layer. The recesses are then filled with enamel and fired. Large areas of the metal can be left as important parts of the design, whereas in cloisonné the metal wires are just for delineation and separation (fig. 54b).

Plique-à-jour
This is a method whereby transparent panels of enamel are held in cells of metal without any backing, so that the finished work has the appearance of stained glass windows. Obviously in this case only transparent enamels are used, to allow the light to pass through (fig. 54c).

Basse-taille
This is a form of champlevé enamelling, except that the design is carved or etched in bas-relief at the bottom of the cell. A layer of

transparent enamel is laid over the whole cell, so that the bas-relief appears in varying shades of the transparent colour covering it (fig. 54d).

Painted enamels

In this case, powdered enamels are mixed with a base medium such as sandalwood or lavender oil and used as paints on a ready-prepared ground of opaque enamel – white if the picture is fairly light, or whichever colour would be most suitable. The whole thing is usually covered in a layer of clear flux when finished.

Like niello, enamelling is the final decorative process to be added to the jewelry and the article must otherwise be completely finished. Enamelled jewelry cannot be added to by soldering, so unless the whole piece is to be fired the designer must consider how the enamel parts are to be attached. They can be riveted or set in a bezel like a stone, or even screwed on. As the firing temperature of the harder enamels is rather high, 850°C (1562°F), any soldering must be done with hard or enamelling solder. Although enamelling solder is specially made for this purpose, I find it rather unpleasant to use. The article being soldered has to be taken to a very high temperature, and on subsequent heatings the joint has a tendency to shrink and become brittle. Hard solder is better because it rarely remelts, and if it does then it runs freely and not in a jagged way like enamelling solder.

Silver, gold, copper and gilding metal may be enamelled. There are also special enamels available for enamelling on steel. Copper should be covered with a layer of clear flux before using transparent enamels, as this prevents the heavy oxidization from interfering with the colours.

The silver used for enamelling may be standard silver or Britannia, although the latter is really too soft for most jewelry. It is possible to buy silver specifically alloyed for enamelling which is very inert and does not react to the enamels.

All joints and catches should be soldered onto the work before enamelling except for those that would lose their tension if reheated, such as box snaps and brooch pins.

It is essential that the work to be enamelled should be absolutely clean and free of grease. In fact, cleanliness is one of the most important factors in successful enamelling, as any particle of grease will prevent the enamel from adhering to the metal and will also interfere with its true colour. The metal should be annealed and pickled, and then scrubbed well with a glass fibre brush or a brass brush lubricated with a weak solution of glue size. The glue size acts as a lubricant, thus preventing a layer of brass being deposited on the silver. It also helps to break up the surface tension. When the article has been cleaned, it can be left in a bowl of water which will keep it clean and prevent dust from settling on the work.

When you are choosing the enamels, try not to have more than four or maybe five colours until you are proficient. Enamels melt at differing temperatures and these are referred to as 'hard' and 'soft' firing, meaning high and low temperatures. Some colours are called 'fugitive', which means that if they are overheated the colour disappears – reds are particularly renowned for this. You cannot mix colours to produce a different shade – each particle remains separate and if you were to mix red and blue you would get, not purple, but red and blue spotted.

The enamels need to be washed and ground every time you use them. Ground enamel can be stored in distilled water for several weeks, but it must be reground and washed before use. To grind the enamel, place it in a mortar (agate mortars are harder than ceramic ones, but in practice ceramic pestle and mortars will usually suffice). Place only as much enamel as you need in the mortar and cover with water. Grind the enamel until it is the size of fine silver sand – experience will teach you the correct size. If you have delicate lines to fill, the enamel will have to be very fine for you to lay it in neatly. During the grinding the water will appear milky, and this is caused by overground enamel and impurities. The water should therefore be changed two or three times during the grinding process. When the correct size has been achieved, wash the enamel until the water runs clear. Even if you buy the enamel as a fine powder, it will still need a little grinding and washing.

Enamel can be laid wet or dry – this process is traditionally known as 'charging'. For anything other than covering large areas (such as plaques for painting metal), it is easier to use wet enamels as they are more controllable. Dry enamels should be sprinkled through a sieve onto the surface of the metal until an even layer has formed. To help the enamel to adhere, a thin layer of gum tragacanth may be painted on the surface of the metal. Although the gum burns away without leaving a residue, I believe it is better to try and manage without any foreign materials as enamels are such a sensitive media. To lay the enamel wet, scoop up a small quantity into a feather quill – this is an extremely useful tool as it enables you to keep the enamel moist, while the point delivers the enamel into the areas to be filled. By pressing more firmly onto the quill, more enamel will be released. Try to ensure that the enamel is pushed into small crevices as they are sometimes overlooked.

Areas are best filled and fired in two or

Silver, ivory and yew conker pendants. Designed by Lexi Dick

three thin layers, rather than one thick layer. By applying thin layers, the stress imposed by the pull of the enamel is more evenly distributed. Any bubbles trapped in the enamel have a chance to escape through a thin layer, whereas the viscosity of a thick layer would prevent this. Although the layers are thin, the metal must be entirely covered as any exposed areas may oxidize and blacken in the kiln – especially if the metal is copper. Dry off any surplus water with a piece of clean cotton rag or blotting paper. All the water must be removed, as any remaining water will boil and cause the enamel to splutter when it is in the kiln. Check that there are no stray grains of enamel on areas of metal that should be clean – they are much easier to remove now with the tip of a wet sable brush than later when they have been fired on.

Support the work on a trivet of any

fireproof material except iron as its heavy layer of oxidization may cause black specks on the enamel if it flakes off during firing. The trivet should be as lightweight as possible so that it does not take longer to heat than the work. Ensure that the work is fully supported, for any projections may sag in the kiln. Carefully place the work in the kiln which should be bright orange/red.

Depending upon its size, the work will take between 1 and 3 minutes to fire. The quicker the enamels are fired, the purer their colours will be. As the work heats up, the enamel will begin to glow and the individual grains will melt and fuse together. Take the work out when it has an orange-peel effect – just before the enamel floods completely. If it is the final layer then it can be allowed to flood. Taking the work out when the enamel is at the 'orange-peel' stage ensures that the work will not be overheated and burnt, and the colours will come up perfectly on the final firing. Cool, pickle and wash the work between subsequent firings. Do not leave the enamel in the pickle any longer than is necessary as soft enamels may be affected by the acid.

As the enamel decorative work is usually level with the surrounding areas, the cells must be slightly overfilled with enamel, which shrinks slightly during firing.

After the final filling and firing, the enamel is ground down until it is level and flat with the metal. Use a clean carborundum stone and grind away the enamel under running water, ensuring that the debris is continually washed away. Do not use a Water of Ayr stone or emery paper as the sludge arising from the use of these materials will collect in the minute bubbles in the enamel, and during the final firing they will burn and appear as black spots. After grinding the enamel will have a matt finish, and it cannot be left in this state as the exposed surface will collect dirt. If a shiny surface is required, the enamel should be refired in the kiln until the surface reglazes. If you would like the kind of matt surface popular with the great Art Nouveau designer, René Lalique, then the work should be refired and dipped in a 50/50 solution of hydrofluoric acid and water. Be very careful when you use this acid as it is one of the most dangerous that you can use. If spilt on the skin no pain is felt but the acid will eat through skin and bone. The fumes are also dangerous. Always wear at least long rubber gloves and a face shield if you have one. Wash your hands carefully afterwards even if you do not think you have any acid on them – and do not forget to rinse the bottle afterwards too. As hydrofluoric acid will eat through glass, you must always use it in a plastic or stainless steel container.

Enamel can be given a low shine by hand polishing. Mix a little zirconium oxide or ceric oxide with water to a thick paste, take a little of this paste up with a felt polishing stick and rub the enamel surface backwards and forwards. Continue to do this, recharging the stick with paste as necessary until a polish is achieved. This is rather a laborious process but the shine is very delicate and soft. The same paste can be used to polish the metal parts. Wash well afterwards.

After the enamel has been given its final finish, all that remains is to polish the metal. If you have polished it well before enamelling, all you should have to do is give it a quick buff with a soft mop and a little rouge – preferably one of the greaseless compounds. If the metal has become marked, it will have to be smoothed carefully with a Water of Ayr stone and repolished. Be careful not to scratch the enamel.

COUNTER-ENAMELLING

Enamel and metal expand and contract at different rates when heated and cooled, which can result in the enamel pinging off or cracking if large areas are involved. Also if a large area is being enamelled, the enamel exerts a pull on the metal, and as the layer becomes thicker so the pull increases until the metal becomes convex. To counteract this a layer of enamel must be put on the reverse side of the metal, and this is known as counter-enamelling. You will only have to counter-enamel if you are going to have large areas of enamel on a flat surface, and experience will teach you when it is necessary.

You can use any colour enamel that you like, and in fact the enamel is commonly made up from a mixture of enamels that have been left over from previous jobs. The layer of enamel is applied by either dry or wet charging, and then fired. The front can now be enamelled, although of course the work must be fired in a support that will not mark the underneath counter-enamel. A springy support of stainless steel can be made to just grip the sides. If no other alternative is available, the work can be balanced on special ceramic tripods which do not stick to the enamel but will just leave tiny pinpricks.

WIREWORK

Decoration in the form of wirework is an important part of jewelry design, and throughout the centuries it has been popular in various forms, as applied decoration or by itself as filigree.

The wires are not necessarily round, and square, triangular or decorated sections may be used. The tools that are needed are few and simple, and in fact it is possible to make complete pieces of jewelry out of wire with a pair of pliers. Some designers base the style of their work completely on the technique of wirework. If you are likely to use wires often in your work, then it is cheaper to invest in a drawplate than to hold considerable stocks of different size wires. A drawplate is a steel plate used to draw large wire down into smaller sizes or to alternative sections (see chapter 2). Buy your silver in a fairly large size, about 1·5 mm ($\frac{1}{16}$ in), as you can always draw down sections of it as you need it.

To draw wire

Anneal and pickle the metal first (see chapter 4 for hints on the annealing of wire). Do not make the mistake of thinking that you can be quick and not bother to pickle the wire, as any dirt or oxides on the surface will be compressed into the metal as you pull it through the drawplate. File a gradual taper about 10 mm ($\frac{1}{2}$ in) long on the end of the wire, so that when it is pushed through the hole in the drawplate it protrudes about 5 mm ($\frac{1}{4}$ in) – enough for the draw tongs to grip easily. If the wire is gold, the taper can be made by hammering the end of the metal rather than filing it, which can be wasteful. Push the wire through the hole of the same diameter and pull it through with the draw tongs – this ensures that any small fluctuations are drawn out. Now proceed down the holes until the correct size of wire is achieved. The wire will need to be reannealed as it hardens, and thick wire will need reannealing more frequently than fine wire. About four to five holes between annealing is a good average. When pulling the wire, try to pull in one smooth operation – jerking or stopping and starting may create small creases which will be weak and liable to break. To assist the wire through the holes, you can lubricate it with a little oil or rub it with wax – this will also help to eliminate

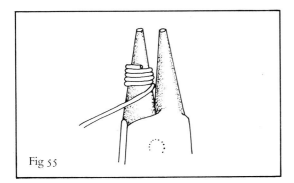

Fig 55

Fig 55 Round-nose pliers can be used to make jump rings

any longitudinal striations which may occur.

When the wire has been annealed, it may be bent to any required design. Make a drawing to the exact size so that you can continually compare the work to the design. To bend wires with pliers, do not attempt to achieve the required shape by squeezing the wires between the pliers as this will only result in ugly marks. Use the shaped jaws of the pliers more like a mandrel by bending the wire against them. To make a tight curve or circle, grip one end of the wire in the jaws of a pair of round-nose pliers, hold the wire between the thumb and forefinger of your other hand and twist the pliers away from your body, at the same time pulling the wire against the pliers.

If you have to make several small rings of equal size, known as jump rings, there are several methods you can use. The first way, and the one that I find the easiest, is to use round nose pliers. Grip the wire in the jaws of the pliers at the point where the diameter of the jaws is the same as the internal diameter of the rings that you require. Holding the pliers with your right hand and guiding the wire with the left, twist your right hand away from your body in a half-circular motion. On the return journey release the wire, which should now have a half curve, and re-grip it slightly farther along the length of the wire. Repeat the forward twist, at the same time making sure that the trailing edge of the wire comes just beneath the first ring, which should now have formed (fig. 55). It will take two forward twists to produce one ring. This is one of those cases where the description takes far longer and sounds more complicated than the real thing!

Another way to form round or other-shaped rings is to use a former, which is just a rod that has the shape and internal diameter that you require. It can be made of hard wood or metal. All you have to do is grip the former in a vice, trapping with it the end of the annealed wire. Then you simply wind the wire tightly around the former (fig. 56).

With both these methods you will be left with a continuous coil of rings. To separate them, simply saw down the length of the coil (fig. 57). The tighter you have wound the

Fig 56 Jump rings can be made by winding wire around a mandrel
Fig 57 Use either a back saw or piercing saw to cut rings

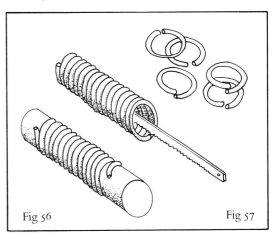

Fig 56   Fig 57

links, the easier you will find it to saw down the length. However, anything much longer than 40 mm (1½ in) becomes unmanageable. If you have a backsaw (a saw which has a thin stiff blade), you will find this easier than a piercing saw. On other than round links, cut where the join will be least noticeable. Do not be tempted to snip through the links with wire cutters, as this tool will squash the ends of the wire and make them difficult to join.

If you are making a chain and want to link several rings together, open the joints by twisting them sideways and slipping the next ring in. This will prevent distortion of the rings. To close the links, firmly press the edges together until they are slightly overlapping – this will make them springy so that when you pull them back they will spring together to make a perfect joint for soldering. (See chapter 6 for hints on soldering chains and links.)

If you want to make several repeats of a fairly complicated wire unit, it will be easier if you make a jig. Draw the exact design onto a block of flat wood. Hammer panel pins into the wood at the points where the wire will have to change direction (fig. 58).

Fig 58 Complicated wire shapes can be formed on a jig

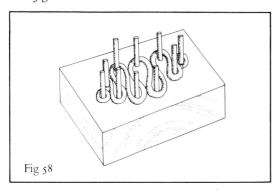

Fig 58

Snip off the heads of the pins when they are in position. Simply wind the wire around the jig and slide it off when complete. Solder the wires at the point where they touch. If the units need to be curved, they can be easily bent at this stage.

Units of wire decoration may be used by themselves or they may be appliquéd onto a metal background. You may wish to mix metals, for example gold wire on a silver background. When soldering wires onto a background, make the paillons of solder minute and place them along the edges where the wire touches the backplate. Heat the whole thing from underneath so that the wires become hot through induced rather than direct heat. This type of decoration looks particularly effective when the background is oxidized and the wires are polished bright (see the section on metal colouring, page 108).

FILIGREE

Filigree is a form of wirework that has been carried to the extremes of intricacy. It is generally most popular in the East, the Indians and the Chinese being particularly adept at this art. It also features as an important aspect of the jewelry of many Mediterranean countries. Although most of the filigree jewelry that we see today has a classical formal arrangement, there is no reason why it should not be used with modern informal designs. Although the following description of the technique is for the traditional designs, it can be used as a basis for any design you may create.

The wire used in filigree must be very fine. It can be made more decorative by twisting or plaiting it and then flattening it slightly by hammering or rolling it through a mill. The design should be divided into small units that are enclosed within larger units. Start by making the largest main pattern. Twist the wires with pliers, taking care to keep the shape flat. Solder this main shape with hard solder so that it is firm. It can now be finished with the inner designs which are usually made of finer wire. The units should be packed in as tightly as possible so that the work is very firm. If the article is to be curved or domed, this is done after the unit is complete as it is practically impossible to keep the units in the correct position if they are curved.

The units should now be soldered to each other and to the main frame. Obviously very fine particles of solder are needed. It is possible to buy easy solder in powder form, but you can easily make fine solder grit by filing a stick of solder with a coarse file and collecting the filings. Borax the complete reverse side of the unit and sprinkle the surface with the solder grit. The work should be soldered by some form of indirect heat, as the flame may easily disturb the light units. A common method is to heat the work in a kiln, taking it out immediately the solder melts. Another method is to raise the work above a charcoal block on a fine mesh support, and to play the flame onto the charcoal block – the heat will rise and melt the solder. When the work has been soldered, it must be pickled and washed as usual. Filigree work usually has only the top surface polished; the sides of the wires are usually left white and matt.

INLAY WORK

Wire can also be used for inlay work, another method of decoration more commonly used in the East where a man's time is still not expensive enough to make the price of a piece of intricate jewelry exorbitant. Almost

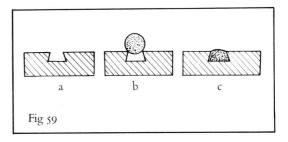

Fig 59

Fig 59a Cut a groove for the inlay into the metal – note the undercut. b Lay soft wire along the groove. c Burnish the wire into the groove

any material that can be cut and grooved can be used as a base for inlay work. Gold, silver, copper, steel, ivory, tortoiseshell and wood are just a few of the materials that have been inlaid. The wires themselves must be made of a soft metal and the two most commonly used are gold and silver. Use 24 carat gold and pure or Britannia silver.

To inlay a line of metal the base material should have a groove carved into it, and the groove should have an undercut edge to retain the inlaid wire (fig. 59a). To cut the groove use either a graver or a reverse cone burr on a flexible drive. First cut or grind down to the required depth and widen the groove at its base. Take a length of soft, round or square wire that is the same width but slightly deeper than the groove. Lay the wire along the groove (fig. 59b) and either burnish the wire into it, or tap it in with a flat-ended repoussé tool and repoussé hammer. File away any excess wire and polish it by burnishing (fig. 59c).

Areas of inlay are treated in much the same way. Cut the design into the base material and slightly undercut the edges. Saw the shape to be inlaid from a piece of metal slightly thicker than the depth of the carved area, and tap in as above. It helps to roughen the bottom of the recessed areas by cross-hatching, which provides a key for the inlay. Dots can be inlaid by simply drilling holes, enlarging the bottom to provide a recess and pushing in the correct-diameter wire. This is known as piqué and was very popular in Victorian times on tortoiseshell articles.

A kind of false inlay can be achieved by gluing the inlay material in the recess in the base material. With this method, materials other than soft metals, for example mother of pearl, can be inlaid into the work. Much Egyptian jewelry was made by this method; slabs of lapis-lazuli or malachite were cut to shape and glued into recessed metal. The Egyptians used a kind of natural lacquer for glue, but today you can use any of the epoxy resins available.

METAL COLOURING

Although the natural colours of metal are attractive in themselves, you may wish for some reason to alter them. Most of the metals used in jewelry can be coloured in some way and old books on jewelry give a variety of recipes for exotic colours. Unfortunately it is very difficult to obtain most of the chemicals that they mention and I have found that many of the recipes do not appear to work, at least not for me. The recipes that follow are ones that I have tested and that really do work. Most of the recipes work better if the water is hot.

The colour most frequently required is black, usually to give an impression of ageing or just to provide a contrast with other areas of metal which may be highly polished. As the colours are only 'skin deep', all polishing should be done before any colouring is attempted. If you make a mistake, the colour can be removed by polishing, or if the colour has got into crevices, the metal will have to be warmed slightly and pickled.

Mix all the components together in a glass or plastic bowl and paint them onto the clean, grease-free metal. Wash the paints off as soon as the required colour has appeared.

To colour copper, silver and 9 carat gold black
1 part ammonium sulphide
2 parts water
If you want a weaker grey colour add more water.

To colour copper brown, and nickel green/brown
1 part copper sulphate
2 parts water

To colour copper purple/ brown, and silver purple/grey
1 part copper sulphate
1 part ammonium chloride
4 parts water

To colour copper green
1 part ammonium chloride
2 parts water
Paint the solution on and leave to dry.

9
Finishing and Polishing

In most instances the way in which you finish your work can 'make or break' it. A sloppy finish will result in a mass of irregularities, through which any fine design will be difficult to perceive. Rounded right angles and wavy straight lines will take away the very basis of crispness and accuracy that a geometrical piece of work requires. Similarly, loose and unrefined curves will destroy the true form of any piece of work. However, do not make the mistake of thinking that an immaculate finish will make a badly designed piece of work any better, though at least it will not compound the faults! Whatever finish you decide to give your work, it must be immaculate.

FIRESTAIN

Before we go on to finishing and polishing, we will have a little word about that bugbear of all jewellers and silversmiths using silver – firestain. Every time silver is heated, unless it is in an oxygen-free atmosphere, the copper content in it oxidizes and builds up as a faint grey layer on the surface of the metal. Beginners find it very difficult to see, even when it is most obvious on a partially polished surface, but it definitely is there and normally has to be removed. The oxide is more obvious when heating copper, as it then presents itself as a thick black flaky layer rather like burnt paper which can easily be

brushed off. On silver the oxide actually forms part of the top layer of the silver and has to be removed chemically or physically.

Pickling after every heating removes some of the oxide, but unfortunately not all. The best way to remove the firestain is by filing or rubbing it away with emery paper or Water of Ayr stone. The metal can then be polished. A heavily textured piece of work can be dipped in a 50/50 solution of nitric acid and water. However, this method is a little unpredictable as the acid may pit the surface and may also attack the solder joints. Any firestain will show as a definite black patch while the metal is in the acid solution – swish the article around until the patches disappear. It is better to do this gradually, continually washing the acid off to check that the metal is not being pitted.

In cases where the firestain can only be removed with great difficulty and damage to the decoration, the whole piece of work may be fired to give a complete layer of firestain all over the work. This will give the silver a greyish-look which is perfectly acceptable, though it can only be done on brooches or similar articles of jewelry that do not wear badly. Rings are not suitable for this process as the silver underneath will become exposed as the firestain wears away.

To fire finished jewelry

The piece of jewelry to be fired should

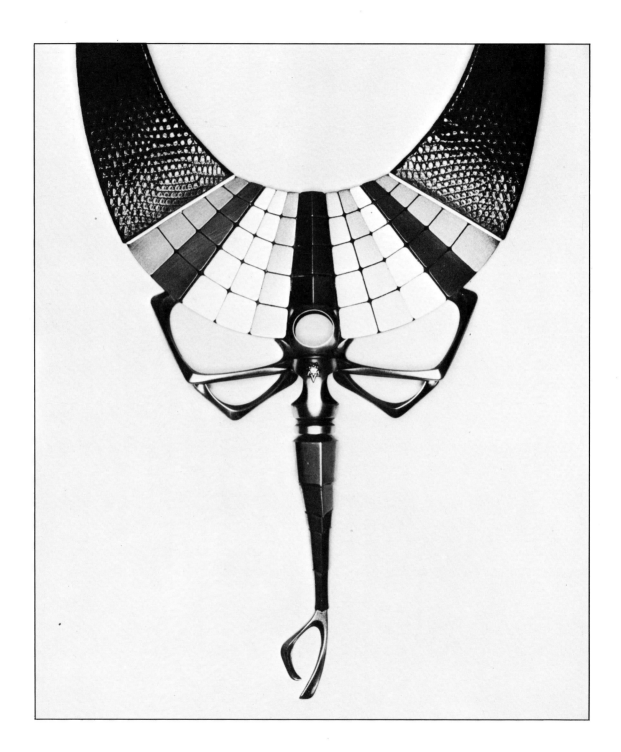

already be finished and polished – except if you are setting stones. Place the work on the hearth and play a yellow smoky flame over it until the article gets very hot but does not glow. Allow the work to cool and repeat the process about five or six times until a thick layer of firestain has been achieved. All that remains is to buff up the final polish with a soft cloth and rouge.

There are some commercial preparations available that can be painted over the entire surface of the work to prevent firestain forming during heating. However, because the compounds are partly composed of flux they encourage solder to run onto surfaces meant to be free of solder and so are really only useful on large pieces of work where the solder joints are far apart. They are usually more useful for the silversmith than for the jeweller.

FINISHING

Finishing is a specialist skill and it is very difficult to tell where finishing ends and polishing begins. In one sense they are just different stages of one process, a graduation through finer and finer abrasive materials. Even the finest polishing compound is really an extremely fine abrasive. However, the two methods are commonly divided at the stage where the abrasives are so fine that an obvious shine occurs.

The article of work should have been filed free of any scratches. If the work has been stamped or etched, then just a final buff with a soft mop should now be necessary, but other surfaces will need to have all the file marks removed. There are various methods

Silver, diamond and snakeskin collar. Designed by David Courts

and materials that can be used to do this. Perhaps the most versatile are the abrasive papers, which commonly fall into two categories – emery papers which can only be used dry, and silicon carbide papers which may be used dry or lubricated with water. Both these types of papers are available in a variety of grades: emery paper numbered from 0 to 4/0, coarse to fine, should be sufficient to cover a jeweller's needs. Silicon carbide papers are available up to about 1200, which is very fine indeed (see chapter 2 for the papers you should buy).

To finish flat surfaces, stick a sheet of the relevant abrasive paper to a sheet of plate glass with double-sided tape. Rub the work backwards and forwards across the complete surface of the paper. Do not attempt to just hold down the paper with your hands because the rubbing motion will make the ends of the paper curl up and catch the edges of the metal, which in time will become rounded. Continually change the direction of the abrasion to prevent furrows being formed in the metal. It is better not to abrase in a circular motion as it makes it rather difficult to see file marks that may be left. Check the work often to make sure the scratches are being removed correctly, and also that you are not accidentally damaging the work by leaning on any of the edges. Continue through the grades of abrasive paper from coarse to fine until a scratch-free finish is obtained – in practice this will mean grade 4/0 in emery paper and at least 800 in silicon carbide paper. Do not try to rush from one paper to another until you are positive that scratches left by the previous paper have been removed. This is a common beginner's fault and will only result in a poor finish and extra work in the long run.

To finish curved or angular surfaces, you will need to use a slightly different method.

You can buy shaped sticks of wood that have emery paper already glued to them. They come as flat, round or triangular sticks and you should choose one to match as closely as possible the surface you wish to abrase. Again, just rub the stick backwards and forwards until all the scratches have been removed. You can make your own sticks instead of buying them. You can also wrap emery paper around files of the correct shape. If you have a flexible drive, a small attachment called a split pin can be purchased. Small strips of paper are inserted into the split and wound around the pin, to form a small cylindrical abrasive tool.

Do not be tempted to rub metal surfaces with a piece of emery paper supported only by your fingers; your fingers are soft and fleshy and will sink into any small depression and rise over bumps, emphasizing the surface irregularities.

A paper called crocus paper is also available and this has a fine covering of rouge. It is so fine that it will impart a shine to the metal and can be used to give a dull, flat finish.

A common and very good alternative to emery paper is a Water of Ayr stone. There are some craftsmen who swear by only one or the other, and you too may find that with time you develop a strong preference – personally I find that on occasions I need to use both. Water of Ayr stone is a natural, grey, soft stone. It is usually purchased in square sectioned sticks varying from 3 mm ($\frac{1}{8}$ in) square to 25 mm (1 in) square. They can be filed to any shape you wish. The stone is used by dipping it into clean water and then rubbing it backwards and forwards across the surface. A slurry will develop as both the metal and the stone are abraded, and as this thickens it should be wiped off or it will clog the action of the stone. Be careful not to pick up grit or metal filings with the stone or you will scratch the metal. When the metal is free of scratches it is ready to be polished.

Very heavily textured or modelled surfaces are a little more tedious to clean. An old traditional method is to use slivers of boxwood and pumice powder as an abrasive – this can be worked into crevices but it takes time. If you have no boxwood, matchsticks and household abrasive powders will do nearly as well. If you have a flexible drive, then there are various attachments you can buy to make the task easier. They fall basically into four categories:

(i) metal burrs
(ii) coarse and fine grinders
(iii) rubber shapes impregnated with abrasives
(iv) polishing brushes, bobs and felts

Only use the pendant drill attachments when it is really impossible for the areas to be finished in any other way – its action is very fast and fierce and unwanted hollows and grooves are quickly formed unless you are extremely careful. If you are right-handed the pendant drill will tend to pull away from the body and to slip off the edge of the work. You can counteract this by pulling slightly towards your body.

POLISHING

By hand
Very beautiful deep polishes can be obtained by hand polishing. This method was used satisfactorily by all ancient jewellers on much the same materials as are used today. Obviously polishing by machine is very much faster and can save a lot of back-breaking work, but machines can also do a lot of damage because everything happens so quickly.

To polish by hand, you will need strips of hard felt and chamois (which should be glued to wooden sticks rather like the emery sticks), hanks of polishing thread and soft wool hand buffs. The basic commercial polishing compounds needed by jewellers are tripoli and rouge. There is a wide range of polishing compounds for different metals (see chapter 2) and, although tripoli and rouge will suffice, it is wise to check if there is a specific compound available for the particular metal you are using. Tripoli is more abrasive than rouge and if the finish on the work is extremely fine already it may not be necessary to use it.

If the work is composed of flat surfaces, you can use the flat polishing sticks. Rub a felt stick liberally with tripoli or, if the surface is very good, with rouge – a few drops of paraffin will help to lubricate the buff. Rub the felt backwards and forwards over the metal, taking care to overlap each stroke and also to change direction to avoid making depressions. Don't 'fall off' the edges of work or they will become rounded. After the metal has been polished well with the felt, graduate to the chamois stick lubricated with rouge, which will give a finer finish. To give the final polish, rub the work with the woollen buff charged with a little rouge. Wash the grease off with detergent, water and a little ammonia. You can if you wish bring up the final shine with metal polish and a soft cloth. To polish the inside of a ring, wrap a piece of leather around a length of round wooden dowel and use this like the other polishing sticks.

Always keep your polishing sticks for the same polish – never mix tripoli and rouge on the same stick. Keep the sticks clean or they will mark your work.

To hand polish a piece of jewelry that has holes or grooves, use a polishing thread. I usually have two hanks of threads hanging from a hook on the edge of my workbench, so that they are readily at hand. Select one or more of the threads according to the size of the hole, spread them liberally with tripoli, thread the string through the hole and rub the work along the string until you raise a polish. Continue with threads covered with rouge. Check your progress because the threads have a tendency to bite into the edges and make grooves. Broader holes can be polished in the same way with strips of chamois leather.

Deep crevices that are inaccessible in any other way may be polished with the rounded tips of hardwood sticks covered with polishing compound. You can finish them off with a cottonwool bud dipped in a proprietary metal polish.

Burnishing
A technique of hand polishing that has a category of its own is burnishing – this relies upon the compression of the surface metal by a smooth tool to give a bright hard polish. Burnishers are made of either highly polished steel or agate, and are available either straight or in a variety of curved forms to suit all shapes. The surface of the tool must have an immaculate polish in order to work properly. To make the burnisher work more smoothly it is commonly lubricated with spit, but if this offends your sense of hygiene use soapy water.

Rub the lubricated burnisher backwards and forwards firmly over the metal surface, overlapping each stroke. To avoid longitudinal lines, burnish across the lines at right angles. A very bright shine will result and with a burnisher it is possible to get into the tiniest crevices. Burnishing also has the effect of hardening the metal by compressing the crystalline structure. This is useful to bear in mind if you have something that is too soft and needs to be hardened, such as a brooch pin or wire necklet.

Machine polishing

Polishing by machine is certainly much faster than hand polishing, and for that very reason you have to be careful as a moment's inattention may do irreparable damage. The polishing speed of the spindle should be about 2500 r.p.m. and will obviously be altered by the size of the mops and wheels that you use – the larger the mop, the faster its periphery will be turning and it is useful to bear this in mind. The most useful size of mop for jewellers is usually 75 mm (3 in). As with hand buffs, you need both hard and soft mops which are charged with tripoli and rouge and which must be kept separately. Make sure the mops are always clean. New swansdown and calico mops should have any stray wisps singed off – besides possible damage to your work, they can give a nasty sting if they whip your fingers while you are polishing. Heavily impregnated mops may be cleaned by running an old coarse cylindrical cheese grater against the rotating mop. Soft mops can be washed in detergent and water.

The position in which you hold the work against the mop is extremely important, and it is both dangerous for your work and yourself to hold it incorrectly. The article should be held firmly, with all your fingers on the outside of it, i.e. when polishing a bracelet do not grip with the fingers inside the band, hold the work only on the outside. This means that in the event of the work being snatched by the mop, your fingers will not be trapped inside. Hold the work against the bottom quarter of the mop and exert a slight upward pressure against the downward pull of the rotating mop (fig. 60). Do not push the top edge or any projection on your

work against the mop, as it will most certainly be snatched away from your hands. Polish from the centre of the work downwards, rotating the work so that the whole surface will eventually be polished. If the work is snatched from your hands, let it go – you can remake your work but not your hands. Long hair should be tied back, and the same goes for ties and flapping garments, though as polishing is dirty work you should wear an overall or smock.

To charge the mops with polish, you just switch on the machine and hold the bar of polishing compound against the rotating mop until it has an even layer all over it. As you polish, move the work so that all the surface is evenly polished – keeping it in one spot can make small areas flat and cause localized over-heating. Continually add polish and always check your work to make sure that you are not wearing anything away. If you have a double spindle, you may find it useful to have a hard mop on one side and a soft

Fig 60 Diagram showing the polishing position. The arrow indicates the direction of the rotation

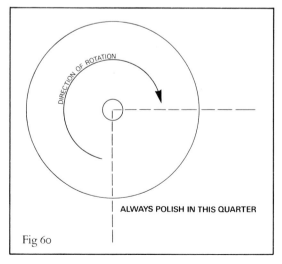

DIRECTION OF ROTATION

ALWAYS POLISH IN THIS QUARTER

Fig 60

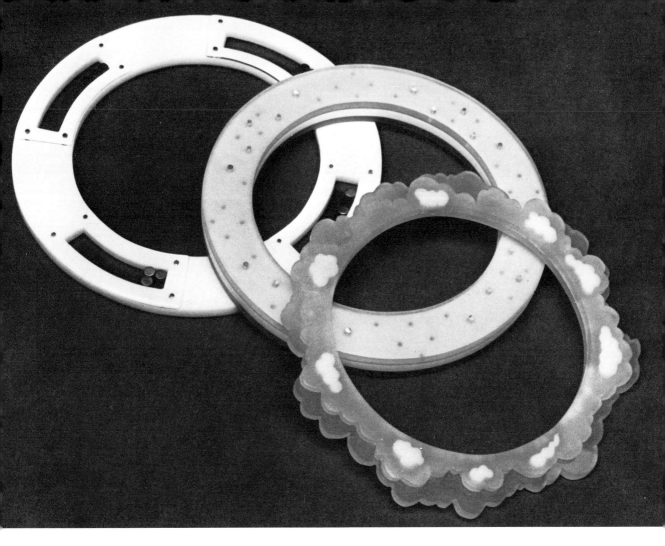

Bangles in acrylic and silver. Designed by Gunilla Treen

mop on the other – the soft mop can be used quickly to wipe away the excess polish on the work so that you can see the progress you are making. Smooth surfaces should be polished first with a hard felt wheel, then a medium calico and then a swansdown mop. Very flat surfaces can be polished on the flat side of the felt wheel, rather than the front curved face.

Textured and decorated surfaces should first be polished with a bristle mop. Use a fairly stiff mop to begin with and then graduate to a soft bristle one, finishing with a swansdown or lambswool mop.

Textured surfaces may also be polished with miniature replicas of the large mops on a flexible drive. Again you must take great care not to make grooves in the metal. It is interesting to note that professional polishers rarely use these small mops, but obtain a high polish on intricate surfaces with the selective use of large mops.

If you want to give your work a satin finish, it is better to give it at least a preliminary shine. A variety of satin finishes can be acquired by using brass or steel bristle mops continually lubricated with soapy water. You must use the soapy water or a brass coating will be transferred to the metal you are polishing. Finer finishes can be obtained by using a bristle mop and whiting. The brush marks should be made in a circular pattern to avoid light and dark patches. A finish known as butler finish is applied simply by rubbing whiting into the surface with your thumb – this gives the soft appearance that old silver has after years of being handled by the butler!

Ivory
To finish ivory, use fine garnet papers and flour paper. Do not use emery paper as the ivory will become stained with a grey powder. Silicon carbide papers may also be used, lubricated with water.

Ivory is polished to seal the absorbent surface which will otherwise stain easily. Hard and soft mops lubricated with tooth-paste and water are used, and you can polish by hand or by machine. If you use a machine, be very careful not to let the mops stay in one place as the ivory will very easily burn from the friction – for this reason the mops must be kept very wet. If you do burn an area, it will have to be removed by filing and the whole process repeated. A little white wax can be rubbed into the surface with a cloth to help seal the pores and protect it from the humidity changes which so easily crack ivory.

Tortoiseshell and amber
These should be abraded with either wet silicon carbide paper or garnet papers. Tortoiseshell will polish easily, using tripoli and rouge or better still one of the household proprietary pastes available for cleaning brass. It can be polished either by hand or by machine, but again great care must be taken not to burn the surface by friction. Use tripoli and rouge for amber.

Abalone and other shells
All nacreous materials should be smoothed by using silicon carbide papers and water. As the surface is very soft, you will have to use a very fine grade – 1200 to get a finish suitable for polishing. Polish the shell with a soft mop and whiting or toothpaste – do not use a hard felt mop at all, as this will strip away the shell's surface. For this reason it is also better to polish by hand rather than risk the fast cutting action of the mop.

Ebony and other woods
Wooden surfaces are usually smoothed with sandpapers and garnet papers. Do not use anything that is wet, such as silicon carbide paper, as this will swell the grain of the wood and make it impossible to smooth. The wood can then be sealed, using either linseed oil or beeswax and a soft cloth. Do not be tempted to use any of the varnish or polyurethane finishes, which may look fine on large pieces of wooden furniture but will kill the subtle beauty needed for the small areas used in jewelry. If wood has been inlaid into metal, smooth the wood but do not wax it. Cover the wooden areas with masking tape and then polish the metal areas – this will prevent the greasy metal polishing compounds from staining the wood. When the metal areas have been polished, the tape may be stripped off and the wood waxed.

Plastics and resins
Perspex, plastic and resin surfaces should be smoothed with wet silicon carbide paper, which will carry away the thick slurry formed by the abrasion of these soft surfaces. As the materials are quite hard to polish, try to achieve as smooth a finish as possible with these papers. For the final polish use a soft mop, either by hand or machine, and one of the proprietary perspex or plastic polishes available. As plastics become static and attract dust, wipe the finished piece of jewelry with an anti-static polish.

10
Casting

Casting is a method of producing jewelry that is very different from most of the other jewelry techniques. In this case the jewelry is made complete and usually in one piece, rarely needing much more work except for polishing. In other words it is a one-step technique, whereas most other jewelry is made in a series of steps and varying techniques. There are many methods of casting, some of which may be done easily with very little equipment, and others which are extremely complicated and usually need expensive equipment. However, it is helpful to know about even the more complicated techniques so that, although you may not be able to do them yourself, you will at least understand the process and will able to have pieces cast by the trade.

CUTTLEFISH CASTING

One of the oldest and most distinctive forms of casting is cuttlefish casting, using the cuttlefish bone as the mould. This method is very easy and cheap to do and an expertise can be developed enabling you to make quite detailed and complex castings. You can cast with silver, gold, aluminium, copper or bronze (the last two require slightly more sophisticated heating equipment). The cuttlefish can be used to produce two different kinds of casting – that which reproduces a master pattern, and that in

which the desired shape is carved directly into the cuttlefish. After the initial preparation both are cast in the same way.

To reproduce a master pattern
Take a large thick cuttlefish and saw it in half widthways with a hacksaw. Rub the soft face of each half completely flat on a sheet of coarse emery paper which has been taped to a flat bench. Put the two faces together to check that they are flat. Now push pieces of matchstick into three or four places around the edge – these will be used to register one face against the other. Take the master pattern (which may be a piece of jewelry that you have already made or another object that you wish to reproduce in metal) and place it in the centre of one of the pieces of cuttlefish. Place the other half on top and squeeze the two together until they meet. Pull the two faces apart and remove the master pattern (fig. 61). You should now have a female mould in two halves, with register holes.

Whatever you use for a pattern should be small enough to leave at least a 9 mm ($\frac{3}{8}$ in) gap between its perimeter and that of the cuttlefish. This is to prevent the heavy weight of molten metal from pushing through the edges when it is poured into the mould.

To carve a pattern
If you examine the soft portion of the cuttlefish, you will notice that it is composed

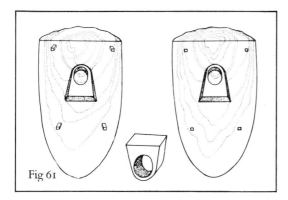

Fig 61 Press the master pattern into the two prepared cuttlefish bones

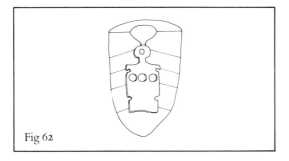

Fig 62 A pattern can be carved into the soft bone

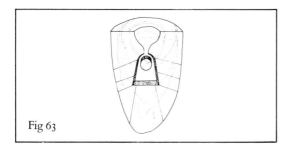

Fig 63 All patterns need a conical pourer carved into the top of the mould and vents for the air to escape

of fine curved ridges of a bony substance interspaced with a soft chalky filling. By brushing away the softer substance to expose the ridges, a beautiful distinctive pattern can be achieved. After you have made one or two castings, you will learn how to make the best use of these lines, much as a woodcarver uses the wood grain to its full advantage.

Prepare the cuttlefish in two flat halves as already described. As it is rather difficult to marry up two halves of a carving, it is better to carve a pattern in one side only and use the other as a flat back. For economy, a charcoal block can be substituted for the backing half, although this means that there will be no cuttlefish pattern on this half. Remembering to leave at least 9 mm ($\frac{3}{8}$ in) at the bottom and sides, carve a design into the cuttlefish, using any tool that will give you the required cut (fig. 62). Thin metal rods are suitable for fine lines and you can shape wooden sticks into tools for larger areas. If you wish to have a hole in the shape, then you must leave that particular area uncarved. Remember that you are working in reverse – deep crevices will be cast as high ridges, and areas that are only cut away a little will result in shallow depressions.

When you have carved out the shape, take a small stiff paintbrush (hog's hair is good) and gently brush the carved surface. As you brush, the soft chalky areas will be removed, leaving the bony ridges exposed. Be careful not to brush the flat face of the cuttlebone where it joins the carving or the molten silver will run across to form flash.

To cast the pattern
See fig. 63. In one half of the bone cut a channel about 6 mm ($\frac{1}{4}$ in) wide leading from the pattern to the top straight edge. Widen and deepen the channel into a cone – this is where the metal will be poured in. With a

fine knife cut lines from the pattern to the edges of the bone to allow air to escape when the airspace in the pattern is replaced by metal. These channels should be only the width of the knife blade or the molten metal may be pushed along them.

Match the two halves of the cuttlefish together and bind them firmly with binding wire – if one of the cuttlebones is longer than the other, cut off the extra at the bottom. Prop the mould upright between two firebricks on a sheet of asbestos in such a way that any molten metal burning right through the mould will not roll off onto your legs.

To melt the metal, place small clean pieces in a boat-shaped crucible – if you have a kiln, the metal may be melted in a cup-shaped crucible in the kiln. Add a good pinch of powdered flux, which will help to keep the molten metal clean and free from oxide. Melt the metal, using either the kiln or bottled gas or a gas/air mixture. When the metal is molten it will look like a squat, bright liquid bead in the bottom of the crucible. If you tip the crucible gently from side to side, the ball should roll evenly. Grasp the crucible in a pair of long-handled tongs, take away the flame and immediately pour the molten metal into the mould. This must be done fairly rapidly to prevent the metal solidifying prematurely. If this is the first time you have poured molten metal, it is a good idea to have a dummy run as a last-minute fumble could be disastrous.

Allow the metal to cool in an upright position for about 5 minutes, then snip the binding wire at the sides to open the mould and allow the metal to cool. This is when your success or failure will be apparent. If it is a failure, the two halves of the mould will give a good indication as to the reasons. If the metal has shot through the bottom or sides, then obviously either the two halves were

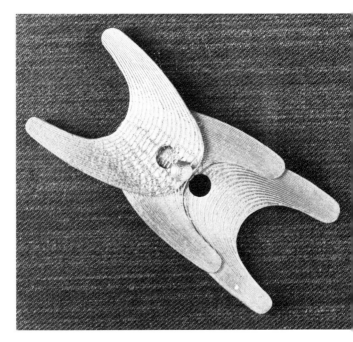

Silver buckle cast in cuttlefish bones. Designed by Charlotte de Syllas

not a perfect fit or the design was too near the edges of the cuttlebone. However, if the metal has only run onto the mould a short distance, check to see that the carving was deep enough to allow the metal to pass – at least 2 mm ($\frac{1}{16}$ in) in the case of silver and gold, and a little deeper in the case of aluminium. If most of the design has been cast but you have odd gaps here and there, check to make sure that there was a route to actually enter that part of the design – as this method of casting relies on gravity. Obviously molten metal will not travel upwards to fill recesses and all entry must be from above the recess. If parts of the design are raised above the main body, then extra pouring channels should be carved into the reservoir.

Clean the design in a sulphuric acid pickle solution and then finish and polish as normal.

LOST WAX CASTING

Today, with the advent of sophisticated machines, complicated castings may be produced singly or *en masse* by lost wax investment casting. If you become very interested in casting, then there is no reason why you should not buy one of the small casting machines that are available. The equipment needed for lost wax casting is as follows:

a vacuum unit to de-aerate the wet investment plaster. You can manage without one of these but it does give a better finish.
a kiln to melt out the wax inside the mould and heat up the finished mould
steel cans for moulds
waxes
a casting machine

If you wish to reproduce a mould then you will also need:
a vulcanizer a press used to make the rubber mould needed to mass-produce a design. It is possible to make moulds from cold-cure rubbers, which would suffice for one or two replicas.
a wax injector used to inject molten wax into a prepared rubber mould

There are a variety of casting machines on the market which work by different methods: centrifugal force, steam pressure and vacuum pressure are the most common ones. The ones most suitable for a jeweller would be a small centrifugal caster or the safer and less dramatic vacuum caster.

The waxes used for modelling are very hard and are capable of taking extremely detailed modelling. The waxes used in the dental trade are those most commonly used by jewellers. They can be supplied in soft sheet form, usually pink, through to a very hard form which is usually blue. The wax comes in sheets, sticks and solid blocks. You can use the softer wax for the basic form and the harder wax for the details.

The tools you will need for modelling are very few and simple. Make your own tools from steel or copper. The best shape is a soft pointed spatula, but practice will dictate the shapes that will be most useful to you. If you have a friendly dentist, ask him for his discarded probes – they make marvellous tools. The wax shape can be carved from a solid block or built up by modelling. Either way, the tool will need to be heated. You can use either a bunsen flame or one of the small methylated spirit burners that are available from jewellers' suppliers. Make sure you always warm your tool in the blue centre part of the flame not the smoky yellow part or you will have sooty deposits in the wax which will mar the surface. The skill in successful modelling greatly lies in the heat of the tool – if it is too cool it sticks to the surface of the wax, and if it is too hot it just melts the wax into an uncontrollable liquid. I am afraid only experience will show you the correct temperature.

Build up the fine details by adding small blobs of wax, allowing each blob to cool before adding the next one – blowing gently hastens the process. To smooth the surface of the finished wax model, burnish it with a slightly warmed tool. The surface of the finished model must be exactly as you would like the metal copy to be – every smear and irregularity will be faithfully reproduced in the casting. If you wish to texture the surface, this can be done at the final stage.

As wax has working characteristics of its own, it is worth experimenting with it to see

Gold rings cast from a cuttlefish. Designed by Jacqueline Mina

exactly what you can do – you may find you like some of the characteristics and would like to use them as direct decoration. For instance, push a very hot tool into a sheet of wax – notice how the molten edge thickens and softens. Try putting two holes next to each other and watch what happens when the two softened edges merge with one another, rather like two bubbles meeting. Let droplets of molten wax form beads on the surface; build up these beads into knobbly stalagmites. There are countless decorative effects that you can achieve.

Another way in which to experiment with wax is to pour molten wax into water. By altering the height and speed of the pour, you will get a wide variety of wax shapes, ranging from gathered round worms to open petal shapes. Try pouring the wax over ice cubes, chunks of cold metal or piles of pebbles and see what shapes you can get. This

sort of accidental designing is sometimes condemned as being uncontrolled, but as long as you exercise some discrimination over the shapes you select or reject I think it is a perfectly valid form of design.

To model a ring
Roll up a tube of paper the same diameter as the ring size, tape the joint well and fold up one end. Pour investment plaster down into the tube and leave it to set – this is a good way of using up any spare plaster, though if you mix it correctly you should not have any waste. Saw off small lengths of this plaster finger and drop them into very hot (not boiling) wax. Leave them in this hot wax until no more bubbles are seen to rise – it takes about 10 minutes. Let the plaster/wax cool and then you can model your ring onto it. When the whole thing is cast, the plaster finger becomes part of the mould and just the wax ring that you have modelled is cast.

An alternative method is to wrap a piece of tissue paper soaked in liquid soap around a piece of tube with the same diameter as the required ring. Model the ring on the top of this soapy paper and when the modelling is complete immerse the wax ring in water – the soap will dissolve and allow you to slide off the model. Any tissue left sticking to the wax can be peeled off.

Before investing the wax model, you will need to determine the weight of metal that will be needed to cast the model. The simplest way to do this is to drop the wax in a glass measuring jar with enough water to cover the model. Mark how much the water level rises, take out the wax model and replace it with clean pieces of the casting metal until the water rises the same height. This gives you the amount of metal needed to cast the model, but you need to add about 10 gm ($\frac{1}{3}$ oz) extra for the sprue and reservoir (see below).

Investing

Select a steel can (these are called flasks, and can be purchased from casting suppliers) which is large enough to contain the model with about $\frac{1}{4}$ in (6 mm) clearance on each side and about $1\frac{1}{4}$ in (32 mm) at the top and $\frac{1}{2}$ in (13 mm) at the bottom – if you use less than this you risk the weight of the molten metal fracturing the mould. Measure the width and length of the can and draw this rectangle on a sheet of paper – this will help you to determine the length of the sprues. Sprues are thin rods of wax which will lead from the pourer to strategically placed points on the model and will be the channels that the molten metal will run along. The sprues should be 1·5 mm ($\frac{1}{16}$ in) in diameter – this is extremely crucial for vacuum casting and pressure casting. Attach the spruces to the outer edges of the wax model (fig. 64). As every model is different, you will have to rely on common sense to tell you where to attach

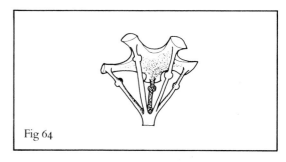

Fig 64

Fig 64 A wax model showing the sprues, each with a blob of wax for a reservoir

them both to the main mass and to any protruberances – imagine metal flowing along the channels and as long as it is not expected to flow upwards against gravity the flow of the metal should be satisfactory. Bring the sprues together and attach them with a good blob of molten wax to the base plate (fig. 65). There are many forms of base plates available; the most sophisticated have rubber seals to attach them to the flask, others

Fig 65 The wax model attached to the cone on a metal base plate

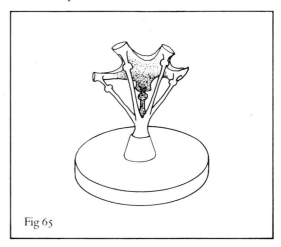

Fig 65

are just flat metal discs with a raised cone in the centre. The cone has a dual purpose – it provides a wide entry hole for the molten metal and also acts as a reservoir for the model to draw on when being cast.

Attach the sprues to this cone. It is very important that the sprues are attached securely. Do not join two cold wax areas with a blob of hot wax, as this will not make a true joint. Instead heat a metal tool and press this between the two wax areas to be joined; when the wax begins to melt withdraw the tool, at the same time pressing the two wax areas together while they cool. This should make a secure joint. Several small pieces of work can be cast at the same time if you arrange them like the spiralling branches of a tree (fig. 66).

Sometimes the area where the sprue joins the body is a little porous after casting, and to help avoid this you can put a small blob of wax just above the start of each sprue (see fig. 64) to act as a tiny reservoir. If the base plate has a rubber seal, just push this onto the flask. If not, then the base plate will have to be sealed with wax to the flask. Make sure you use a fairly thick wedge; the soft beeswax is the best kind for this. The joint must be well sealed. Rinse the flask and model with soapy water. This serves two purposes. It tells you if the joint is watertight and the soap also breaks down the surface tension of the wax, allowing the investment plaster to adhere to every crevice and detail. If you are going to use a vacuum unit to suck out surplus air, then tape a paper collar around the neck of the flask extending at least 8 cm ($3\frac{1}{4}$ in) above the edge, because during the air extraction the investment rises and may spill over.

There are many types of investment plaster available – for jewelry choose one of the very fine ones. The supplier will be able to give you advice. Each manufacturer will

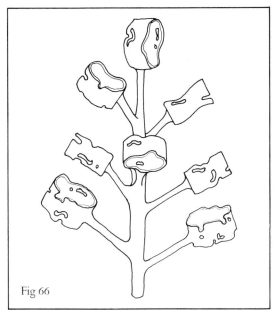

Fig 66

Fig 66 Small items such as these rings can be cast together like a tree

recommend mixing instructions for his particular investment and these should be followed closely. However, as a general rule the mixture should resemble double cream, thin enough to pick up the finest detail but thick enough to adhere to the wax. For economy, you can if you wish paint a thick layer of fine investment over the mould and fill the rest of the can with a coarser investment. If extra time is needed for the investment to set, then a few drops of retarding agent may be added to the investment. If you are not using a vacuum unit, you can add a few drops of a defoaming agent, though this is not vital. When you have mixed your plaster, pour it carefully into the flask, allowing it to settle as you pour. Use a fine brush to push the investment into crevices. When full, leave it to set or

place it in a vacuum unit and de-aerate for 30 seconds or as instructed by the plaster manufacturer. The plaster will rise up inside the paper band you have added, and when the vacuum is normalized it will subside.

When the plaster has set, carefully remove the base and check that the wax sprues are visible as single sprues. If they are clustered together, scrape away a little of the wax and plaster until the sprues are isolated – this is particularly important for steam and vacuum castings. Peel away the paper collar and make sure the plaster is level with the flask; if not, then scrape away the surplus plaster.

Place the flask, pourer side down, inside the cold kiln. Heat the kiln up gradually, allowing the wax to melt out – this should take about 1 hour. Turn the kiln up to 800°C (1472°F) and leave the flask to heat up until it glows red when you look into the interior of the mould; if it looks at all black, then it is not ready. If you cannot control the temperature of the kiln, place the flask in the open doorway of a red-hot kiln and, turning the flask frequently, leave it until the wax has burnt out, then place it inside the kiln until the interior glows red. The mould can then be cast by any of the following methods.

Casting by centrifugal force

Place the hot flask in the cradle and the crucible and metal at the other end of the balance. Adjust the weights so that the crucible balances against the flask. Tension the balance according to the manufacturer's instructions – this normally means rotating the arm once and securing it with the catch. Now add flux to the clean metal and heat it with propane or a gas and air mixture until the metal melts and resembles a silver liquid.

Melted silver and bezel set cabochon stones. Designed by Gerda Flockinger

When you are sure the metal has melted, release the catch and allow the balance to swing round. The whole operation is very dramatic and it is advisable to stand well back in case of accidents – most people hit the release catch with a hammer at arm's length. As the arm begins to slow apply the brake, and when the arms begin to stop jerkily, hold the balance with the mould at the bottom – this should happen naturally because the weight of the flask now has the additional weight of the metal, but I have seen the flask trying to defy gravity so it is better to stop it at the bottom rather than have molten silver pouring back out of an upside-down mould. Allow the flask to cool for about 5 minutes, then quench it in a bucket of cold water which will break the plaster away from the cast metal. Pickle the cast well; you may need to heat it to get it really clean. You can, if you wish, remove tiny bits of stubborn plaster with hydroflouric acid but, in view of the dangerous qualities of this acid, I prefer to just scrub it well with a wire brush.

Vacuum casting

Vacuum casting is one of the newer methods of casting on the market and it is, I believe, by far the safest and least dramatic of all the methods. In vacuum casting, air is first removed by means of a pump from the barrel of the casting unit with the valve at the side closed. There is also a valve in a hole on the top plate of the unit and a pad of ceramic fibre or any other fireproof material is placed over the top of this plate. (The pads are available from the unit's manufacturer.) Place the hot flask on top of the pad, with the pourer cavity side up. Put the clean scraps of metal in the pourer together with a little borax and melt it with propane or gas and air mixture. When the metal has melted, release the valve at the top and the vacuum inside

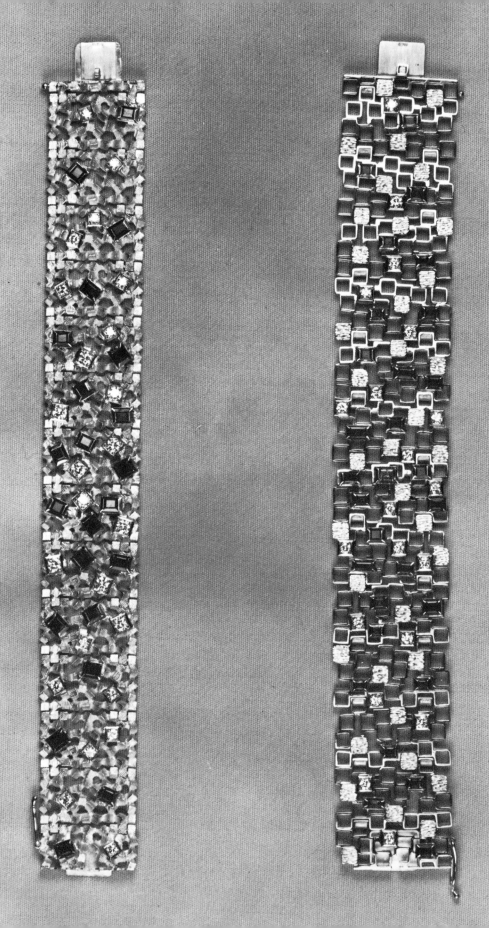

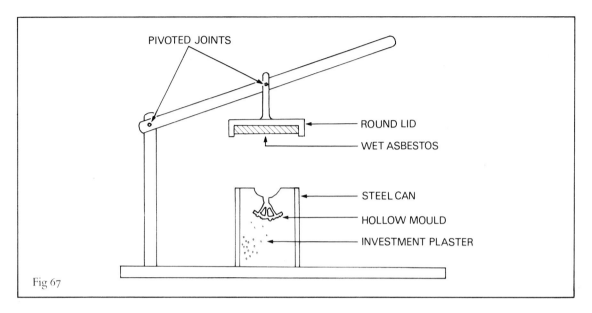

PIVOTED JOINTS

ROUND LID

WET ASBESTOS

STEEL CAN

HOLLOW MOULD

INVESTMENT PLASTER

Fig 67

Fig 67 A steam caster showing the plaster mould in position

sucks up through the hole and through the plaster to draw the molten metal down into the mould. You can see the metal disappear down quite easily. Switch off the pump and allow the flask to cool, and expel excess air through the side valve. As mentioned earlier it is very important that the sprues are exactly 1·5 mm ($\frac{1}{16}$ in) in diameter – if they were larger, the molten metal would start to run down into the mould before the valve had been opened.

Steam casting

In some ways this method is similar to vacuum casting, except that the metal is

Two bracelets, 18 carat gold, diamonds and garnets. Designed by John Donald. Both these bracelets were made by casting – note the box catch fastening

pushed rather than sucked down into the mould. The steam caster has a wad of wet asbestos held in a cup halfway down an articulated arm. Place the hot flask on the stand and test that when the arm is brought across, the pad will fall exactly on top of the flask. Try this without the asbestos. It is very important that the flask is exactly in place, for if the pad catches just the edges, the flask will fall over and spill the molten metal. Now fill the cup with wet asbestos. Melt the metal in the pourer cavity, as described above under Vacuum casting. When it has melted, quickly bring across the arm and push the wet asbestos onto the flask. The hot flask and asbestos will generate steam, which will push the molten metal down into the mould. Again the sprues must be only 1·5 mm ($\frac{1}{16}$ in) in diameter or the metal will trickle into the mould before you are ready (fig. 67).

There are other, less popular methods of casting that you may hear about. By all means try them, as you may find a method that suits you particularly well.

Set of rings in 18 carat gold and gems, designed to
be worn in groups. Designed by Wendy
Ramshaw

11
Stone Mounting
and Setting

Stone mounting and setting are specialist skills and in the short space of a chapter only the rudiments can be covered. If you need to know more than the basics, you should consult a book entirely devoted to this subject.

Mounting and setting are two separate techniques: mounting covers the actual construction holding the stone, and setting applies to the permanent enclosing of this stone within the construction. Stone mounting is really a matter of small-scale engineering. You have to find a way of holding a stone onto a piece of jewelry in such a way that it cannot move sideways or fall out once you have set it. It is interesting to look at the many ways that stone mounting has been approached, from the traditional to the purely engineering.

The oldest, simplest and most commonly used setting in modern jewelry is the bezel setting (fig. 68a). This is basically a thin band of metal soldered to the main body of the jewelry with the top edge turned over to hold the stone. The first step in constructing a bezel is to make the band that goes around the stone. This needs to be quite thin, about 6 BMG (0·4 mm), as metal any thicker will be difficult to turn over. If the mount is to be made in silver you will find it even easier if the bezel is made of Britannia silver, though this is not vital.

The height of the band will depend on the type of stone being set. Some stones have to

be set resting on a bearer wire which is soldered inside the band – this applies mainly to faceted stones or stones which have an uneven bottom. It can also be used if you wish to raise the stone considerably above the height of the main body of the jewelry. The bezel should be just high enough to hold the stone securely – very high stones need more height than flat-topped stones. You can get a rough idea of the length of the bezel needed by wrapping a piece of paper around the stone. Cut the required length and height of bezel. If you are unsure of the height make it a little too large; it can easily be trimmed later. Anneal the band and shape it with pliers to fit the stone exactly – if it is too large, ugly creases will form as you try to set it. If you have difficulty making the bezel fit the stone exactly, make it slightly smaller and then stretch it to fit by hammering it on a triblet. This is easy to do with a round stone but considerably more difficult with a square one. To test the fit, always drop the stone gently into the bezel and not the other way around – as the band is still flexible it will change shape to accommodate the stone, and it will be difficult to tell if the bezel really fits.

Solder the ends of the bezel together with hard solder (fig. 68b). If the bezel is square, make the joint on a corner where it will be most unobtrusive. Check again to make sure the stone still fits. Next solder the bezel onto the main body of the piece of jewelry,

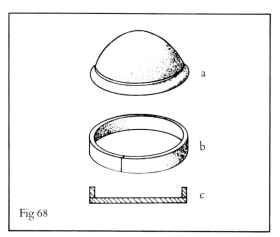

Fig 68

Fig 68a A simple bezel setting. b Make the bezel fit the stone exactly and solder the joint. c Solder the bezel to a back plate

placing the paillons of solder inside the bezel. If the mount is to be a complete part of the jewelry, as for example a brooch, then the bezel should be soldered onto a slightly larger backing sheet and the excess filed away (fig. 68c). The sheet should be thicker than that used for the bezel, to make it stronger. Further refinements and economies can be made by piercing out some of the backing sheet to let in light and save metal.

If you should try the stone before you are ready to set it and find that it becomes stuck, place stone and mount inside a wooden or cardboard box and shake hard – the stone should fall out. Another method is to stick a wedge of plasticine onto the stone and try to pull it out. The final resort is to drill a small hole in the backing sheet and push the stone out from behind.

All that remains is to turn the top edge of the bezel over the stone – this is not done until all the work on the piece of jewelry is complete as most stones cannot be subjected to any heat. The bezel edge can be pushed

over the stone in several ways. If the metal is soft and thin, it can be burnished over with a steel or agate burnisher. Slide the burnisher along the edge, pressing down firmly at the same time. To ensure that the stone is held evenly, start by pressing the burnisher down at opposite points and then continue to press down the metal in between. With square or rectangular settings, you should file away a small V-shaped notch at each corner so that the setting will lie down neatly, or you will find you have little 'ears' sticking up. If the bezel is too hard or thick to be bent down by burnishing, it can be turned over using a pusher or by tapping the edge (fig. 69). A pusher is a length of square-sectioned steel, about 4 mm ($\frac{1}{8}$ in), held in a graver handle. The edges of the pusher should be softened and the whole face polished. The bezel should then be turned over by pressing the pusher inwards and downwards on the top edge. Start by pressing down at an angle of about 45°, raising your hand gradually until it is pressing down almost vertically onto the bezel edge. This movement should be carried

Fig 69 Bezels can be closed with a pusher like this by simply pressing on the sides at an angle of 45°

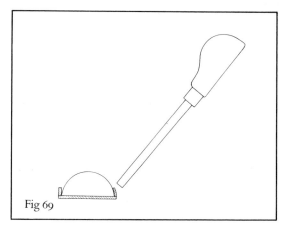

Fig 69

Fig 70

Fig 70 To make setting easier, work may be held in a setting stick

out quite quickly. Again start by securing the stone at four opposite points.

Using a setting tool and hammer is rather similar to the pusher, except that instead of being held in a handle the metal tool is tapped down with a chasing hammer, giving a tight, smooth setting. Again the edge is turned over by tapping the tool at an angle of 45°, gradually raising the tool until the edge is being pressed down vertically. Secure at four opposite points as before. To finish the setting, smoothly tap the tool, rapidly but gently, while letting it slide along the bezel.

With all these methods of setting it is essential to try and get as smooth a finish as

possible without resorting to using a file. If you should have to file the finished setting, use your thumbnail to protect the stone where it meets the bezel as many stones are easily damaged by filing or emery paper. If the stone is porous – turquoise, malachite, coral or pearl, for example – polish the bezel by burnishing it. Only if the stone is hard may the bezel be polished with rouge, which would discolour porous stones. For all these setting methods, especially the last one, you will probably need two hands so the work is best held on a setting stick. This is a length of wooden dowel about 25 mm (1 in) in diameter and about 150 mm (6 in) long with a large ball of setting wax on the end (fig. 70). Setting wax is a kind of shellac rather like sealing wax which can be softened with a gentle flame. Support the work by pushing it into the ball of softened wax – in the case of a ring, the whole shank should be buried with only the mount exposed. The wooden dowel can then be gripped in a vice, leaving both hands free to set the stone. To take the work out, warm the wax gently with a flame taking great care not to let the work become warm, prize the softened wax away from the metal and pull the work out. Any residue of wax can be removed with acetone or methylated spirits.

BEZEL SETTINGS WITH BEARER WIRES

It may be necessary to use a refinement of the basic bezel setting by placing a bearer wire inside the bezel. This is used whenever the stone needs to be lifted above the base of the mount, for instance when the stone does not have a flat bottom or when the bezel has to be soldered onto a curved surface such as a ring shank (fig. 71). In this case the bezel needs to be extra deep so that a curve may be

131

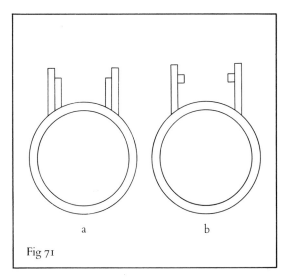

Fig 71

Fig 71a Section showing a ring with a bezel setting and a bearer collar inside to lift up the stone and prevent it from rocking on the rounded ring shank.   b A similar ring with a bearer wire

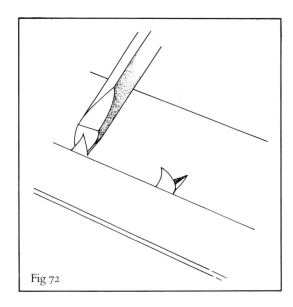

Fig 72

Fig 72 Push a square graver into the metal and push up a sliver of metal to make a stitch

filed into the base to correspond to the curve of the shank.

A bearer can be either another complete band set down inside the bezel or a fine wire ring. It is possible to buy ready-manufactured bearer wire which has a small ledge cut into it to support the stone. If the base of the bezel and the bearer are to be level, then it is a simple matter of making a slightly smaller band of the required height and soldering it inside the bezel. However, if the bearer is to be a wire soldered at a specific height within the bezel then the procedure is a little more complicated. Make the wire bearer fit tightly within the bezel. With a pair of dividers, mark the height at which the top of the bearer must be soldered. If the bearer fits tightly, align it with the mark and solder it in. Sometimes it is difficult to make the bearer stay at the correct height and in this case a few 'stitches' will make the task easier.

Stitches

Stitches are small prongs of metal cut from the bezel with a graver – on which the bearer will rest. It is useful to know how to do them as they can be helpful in many other tricky fitting operations (fig. 72). To make the stitches, measure the thickness of the bearer wire. Scribe another line this thickness below the other line you have already marked inside the bezel. Take a graver and push steeply into the metal just above the top line. When you reach the second line, push the graver handle upwards so that the sliver of metal you have just cut projects out at right angles to the inside face of the bezel. You have now made a little ledge on which to rest the bearer wire. Make several of these stitches around the inside of the bezel until the bearer can be evenly supported and soldered in. The stone can then be set by any of the methods already outlined.

Silver, ivory and opal brooch. Designed by Kay Dowding. The opal 'pool' is secured by a bezel

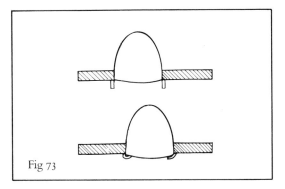

Fig 73 A stone set from behind. Claws or a bezel can be used to secure the stone

BEZEL SETTINGS FROM BEHIND

Bezel settings are used to set steeply sided stones from behind, giving a kind of invisible setting. The metal for the setting needs to be thick enough to hold the stone. Cut a hole smaller than the base of the stone, then file it to an angle corresponding to the sides of the stone until the stone drops neatly into the hole with the base projecting about 0·5 mm. Solder either a narrow bezel or claws around the edge of the hole and use these to secure the stone (fig. 73).

ROMAN SETTINGS

These look rather like a thick bezel setting and have a very strong appearance (fig. 74). They can only be used on stones which have sloping sides and are usually reserved for flat-

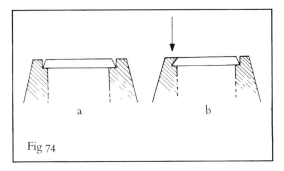

Fig 74a Roman setting. Carve a ledge into thick metal. b Compress the metal downwards and inwards to hold the stone

topped stones. The stone rests on a bearer which can either be soldered in or carved from the thickness of the metal, using either a graver or a burr on a flexible drive. When the stone fits perfectly on the bearer inside the hole, tap vertically downwards with a setting tool, compressing the metal both outwards and inwards over the stone. The surplus metal on the outside edge can be filed away, leaving the interior edge to hold the stone.

133

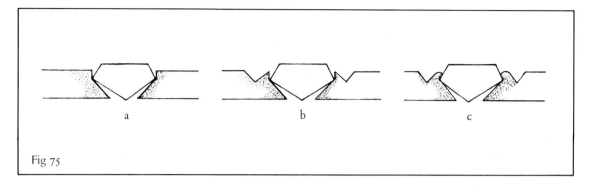

Fig 75

Fig 75a Pavé setting. Grind out a hole the correct size with a setting cone. b Throw up claws with a graver. c Press the claws down on the stone to hold it securely

PAVÉ SETTINGS

This is a method in which small-faceted stones are held onto the surface of the metal by small claws cut from the edge of a hole without actually making a formal claw setting (fig. 75). A small hole is drilled where the stone is to be set, and opened out with a special burr called a setting cone that corresponds to the diameter of the stone. The stone can then be dropped into the hole. Small points rather like stitches are thrown up by a graver at even points around the circumference of the stone. Using grain tools, the stitches are then rounded and compressed tightly onto the edge of the stone to hold it in place.

CLAW SETTINGS

Claw settings are used mainly to hold faceted stones. They allow light to pass through the setting, thus enhancing the brilliance of the stone. This type of setting can be bought very easily in a wide variety of designs and they are only worth making yourself if you want something individual or an odd shape. The following designs are traditional ones which can form the basis for any modern variation. You can make the claws irregular in shape and design to suit your particular piece of jewelry.

The simplest form of claw setting for holding very small stones is two V shapes soldered together at their bases. The point at the base can then be filed flat and soldered to the main body of the jewelry. Small ledges are then cut out of the inside of the claws slightly below where the girdle (widest part) of the stone is to rest. The ledges can be cut with a graver or a sharp burr on a flexible drive. Push the stone down until it snaps into a recess formed by the ledges. The claws are then pushed over the top of the stone with a burnisher or graining tool (fig. 76).

Fig 76 A simple four-claw setting with ledges cut to hold the girdle of the stone

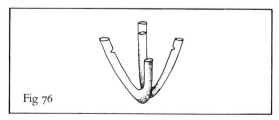

Fig 76

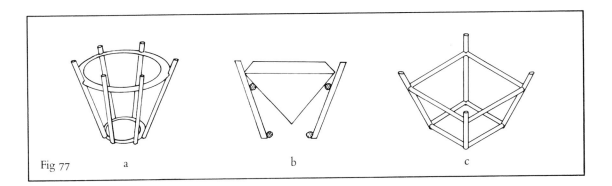

Fig 77   a   b   c

Fig 77a A six-claw round wire setting.   b Cross-
section of the stone inside the setting.   c A four-
claw square setting

For larger stones more complicated and
secure methods must be devised. Fig. 77
shows a round and square setting. The square
setting is usually referred to as a box setting.
Although in these particular designs round or
flat wires have been used for the claws, any
cross-section of wire may be used, bearing in
mind the general character of the design.

Using pliers and wire of your choice, make
up a ring or rectangle that is slightly smaller
than the girdle of the stone. When the
stone is dropped into the ring it should
rest with the girdle just above it. Then make
a smaller ring which will be the base of the
setting. Mark the ring with the number of
claws you are going to need – usually six or
eight. With a file, make small grooves at
these points halfway through the thickness of
the wire. As these grooves are to hold the
wire claws, they must be of the same shape as
the wires; thus, for round wires use a round
file and for square wires use a square file.

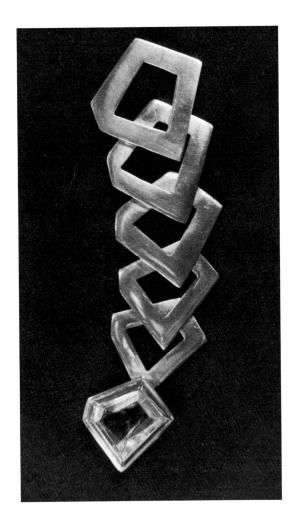

Silver and aquamarine brooch. Designed by Jean
England. Each shape of this brooch is articulated
by hinges. The stone is set in a bezel with the back
pierced away to let light in

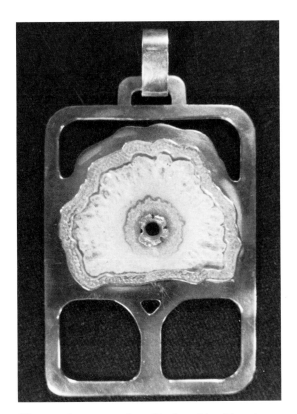

Silver and agate pendant. Designed by Maggie Linden. The design of this pendant has been strongly influenced by the interesting shape of the agate slice which is secured by its centre

Measure the distance between the girdle and culet or point of the stone with a pair of dividers. Take a small piece of wet asbestos paper or soldering plasticine and mould it into a small cone shape slightly larger than

Pendant designed by Catherine Mannheim. Silver background textured by melting the surface, cameo photograph mounted in a bezel, and 18 carat gold appliquéd feather and photograph mounts

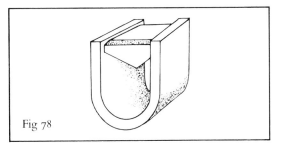

Fig 78 A modern tension setting

the stone. Dry this cone with a flame until all the water has evaporated. Push the larger of the two rings down onto the cone, leaving a gap of about 1·5 mm ($\frac{1}{16}$ in) between the base and the ring. Push the smaller of the rings onto the cone until the gap between the two rings is the distance that you measured with the dividers. Align all the grooves between the two rings. Prop the small lengths of wire claws in the grooves resting against the cone and solder them in. In effect the setting is being made upside down. The setting should be tidied and then the recesses cut and the stone set as described for the simple claw setting.

A relatively modern concept for setting stones is to hold them under tension. For example, a square stone might be held between the two opposing sides of a tensioned U shape (fig. 78). This U shape could be adapted to hold almost any stones – balls, cubes or whatever. However, it can only be done really successfully with one of the hard golds as most other metals lose their tension too quickly. This sort of design provides a refreshing contrast to the more traditional settings and is an indication of how ingenuity can create really different answers to a common problem.

Further Reading

Choate, Sharr and De May, Bonnie Cecil
Creative Gold and Silversmithing
George Allen and Unwin, London 1971

Hughes, Graham
The Art of Jewelry
Studio Vista, London 1972

Modern Jewelry
Studio Vista, London 1968

Von Neumann, Robert
The Design and Creation of Jewelry
Pitman, London 1973

Untracht, Oppi
Enamelling on Metal
Pitman, London 1957

Wilson, Harry
Silverwork and Jewelry
Pitman, London

Index

List of designers